D0271314

FLORISTRY HANDBOOK

Rona Coleman

B T Batsford Limited   London

Acknowledgment

The author acknowledges with thanks:
Eric Roberts, NDSF, a great teacher, for the diagram on page 52.
Jacqueline Elgood who patiently checked the first proofs.
Stanley Coleman, who has made numerous valid contributions to the contents of this book as well as taking some of the pictures.
Joan Pare, NDSF, for the lovely asymmetrical bridal bouquet illustrated on page 93.

© Rona Coleman 1986
First published 1986
Reprinted 1987, 1989, 1991, 1992

Typeset by Servis Filmsetting Ltd, Manchester
and printed in Great Britain by
Butler & Tanner Ltd
Frome, Somerset
Published by B T Batsford Limited
4 Fitzhardinge Street, London W1H 0AH

British Library Cataloguing in Publication Data

ISBN 0 7134 5143 2

Coleman, Rona
    Floristry handbook.—(Vocational handbooks)
    1. Flower arrangement
    I. Title   II. Series
    745.92   SB449

Contents

1 **Introduction to the flower industry** 5
Tools 6
Working clothes 7
Refreshments 7
Areas of responsibility 7

2 **Wires and general equipment** 9

3 **Basic design** 15
The technical 16
The visual 19
Shapes for colour harmony check 21

4 **Wiring methods** 27
Flower form groups 28
Stem texture groups 28
External wiring 29
Internal wiring 31
Rose pinning 34
Unit assembly 38

5 **Arrangements** 40
Definitions 40
Objectives 41
Equipment and planning 41
Facing arrangements 44
All-round designs 45
Asymmetrical arrangements 46
Hospital arrangements 48
Parallel form 48
Decorative form 49
Vegetative form 49
Using tubes and candles 50
Anniversaries 51

6 **Funeral tributes and sympathy designs** 54
Types of bases and frames 54
Mossing 55
Informal tributes 55

7 **Funeral tributes: formal designs** 61
Edging 61
Backing 64
Formal designs on mossed bases 66
Open based designs 70
Laurel pinning 75

8 **Buttonholes, corsages and head-dresses** 78
Buttonholes for lady and gentleman 78
Corsages 80
Prayerbook spray 81
A unit 82
Circlet head-dresses 82
Everlasting flowers and foliage 83
Bouquet bases 84

9 **Weddings** 85
Bouquet handles 85
Suggested work programme 86
Classic or shower bouquet 89
Semi-crescent design 90
Full crescent bouquet 91
Bascade or baskette 94
Open posy 96
Duchesse or carmen rose 97
Bride cake top 98

4 *Contents*

Victorian posy 99
Pomander 100
Outside decorations 101
Church arrangements 101

**10 Window dressing and
display 107**
Objectives 107
Practical basics 109
Price tickets 109
Guidelines 110
Special displays 110
Lighting 111
Designs 112
Window shopping 112

**11 Care and conditioning of
perishable stock 113**
Care of stock, general 114
Cut flowers 114
Stock conditioning,
general 114
Special subjects 115
Foliages 119
Dry pack 120
Cool storage 120
Flowering and foliage
plants 120

**12 Packing and
presentation 125**
Cut flower packing 126
Cellophane presentations 126
Ribbon finishing 127
Packing container designs 130

13 Daily work routine 137
Pre-planning and
delegation 137
Delivery lists 139
Order checking 140

Reservation of material for
designs 142
Conditioning flowers and
foliage, and care of plants 142
Shop and telephone sales 142
Window and shop display 143
Routine cleaning 144
Lunch breaks 144

14 Organising deliveries 146
Planning the route 146
Timed and untimed
deliveries 147
Specimen delivery sheets 147
Non-delivery 148
Vehicle responsibility 149
Vehicle service 151

15 Customer relations 152
Dealing with complaints 154

16 Staff relations 157
Basics of good staff
relations 158

**17 Peak period
organisation 163**
Record keeping 163
Publicity 164
Key points 165
Self-preservation 169

18 Salesmanship 171
The choice 172
Sales persuasion 173
Special occasion selling 174

19 Peak trading days 177

20 Questions and answers 179

Index 182

1 Introduction to the flower industry

What exactly is floristry? In essence, it involves preparation and presentation of cut flowers and foliage ready to sell in the shop. It embodies understanding how to make arrangements, bouquets and funeral tributes, for a good florist is an efficient technician as well as being a capable salesperson.

Many flower shops are relatively small units, some being run by one person with part-time help, while others involve the family or, perhaps, a husband and wife team. Thus, the up-to-date florist needs to be something of a jack-of-all-trades but very definitely master of all of them if the shop is to succeed.

The florist is working all the time with living materials. Factors such as availability of material, prices, seasonal fluctuation, how to condition, how to store and when to use, what is most suitable for this or that design, all these must be fully understood. Fascinating subjects, every one of them, but there is really no quick way to learning it all. Rather, a firm basis of technical know-how should be gradually expanded season by season, which will ultimately add up to valuable experience. For experience is defined as an actual observation of facts or events; in other words, what you see for yourself rather than what you are taught as a student.

Forty years ago, the only way to learn to be a florist was to be taken into a workroom and learn what you could, when you could, by watching people at work. A slow and painful process, yet it must have had some appeal, otherwise there would be no enthusiastic florists today.

Now, as time rushes forward to the twenty-first century, good training is vital. Floristry, both technically and artistically, has reached exciting peaks of quality and expertise. But this need not imply that only the artistically-endowed will succeed. For the basics of a good florist involve a respect for the living material –

flowers and plants – tremendous energy, good health, discipline and dedication, a liking for people and a cheerful disposition.

If you are fortunate enough already to have had some formal training you will, of course, understand most of the operations of the workroom, but for someone without this background, the first few days could be rather baffling.

Every industry involves processing raw materials to some stage before they can be offered for sale. The flower industry is no exception. Cut flowers arrive in the shop, perhaps from local growers, possibly by air from the other side of the world, and they must all be cared for expertly before they are used in designs or sold as cut flowers to the public.

For the first few days, maybe even weeks, you may not be asked to handle any of the flowers. However, do not be downhearted, for conditioning the fresh stock is a very responsible part of the florist's work.

Equip yourself with a notebook so that you can record the names and varieties of flowers as they come in, how they are cared for and how they are used. You will be amazed how quickly these notes will increase, building up to an exciting year-round diary full of season-by-season information.

Tools

A **notebook** and **ball-point pen** are essential. Choose the type of pen that can be operated with one hand, rather than the kind with a cap. They are quicker to use and there is no cap to fall off and get lost.

You will certainly need a **sharp knife**; this is not an expensive item. One of the best is a little one with a bright orange handle, costing less than a pound and which can be sharpened as necessary. It has a fixed blade so is not very safe to carry in the pocket, but when not in use the point can be driven into a cork.

One or two points are worth remembering when choosing your **scissors**. Naturally, they must cut florists' wire and ribbon. This seems a tall order but such scissors do exist and it is far quicker to be using only one pair for everything. The scissors must be well-balanced and comfortable to hold. You may prefer to try one or two less expensive designs before making your final decision. The better ones are expensive and should last several years.

Keep your own set of tools – scissors, knife, pen and duster and never borrow other people's. It is most frustrating to find your scissors being used by someone else at the very moment you need them.

Working clothes
During your initial interview with your employer, you will probably have discussed the type of **overall** or jacket to wear. Some of the smartest firms have house colours and a logo, so that all staff present a uniform appearance to the public. This also creates an excellent publicity effect, for when some of the team are working on an outside decoration the public naturally identifies a particular colour-scheme with one particular shop.

Whatever the firm's policy it will probably be your responsibility to keep your overalls crisp and clean. Wear **comfortable shoes** for you will be standing for most of the day. Be prepared to work in a relatively cool atmosphere, colder that is, than at home or in an office. If you need an extra jacket or pullover, wear it *under* your overall. Try never to wear it outside as the general effect is most unprofessional.

Refreshments
If you go from training college or school direct into a workroom it will be a very sudden change for you. You will be standing or moving about for most of the time and it is likely that you will be far more hungry than usual. So take an extra snack for lunch and tea break otherwise you may find yourself drooping long before closing time.

Areas of responsibility
In the early days of your career as a florist no employer will expect you, as a student-florist, to understand the routine and all about the flowers and equipment at once. However, do make sure you understand whatever you are asked to do before you begin. It is far more aggravating if a student pretends to comprehend and goes ahead to complete a particular operation all wrong. This results in loss of valuable time and equipment. You are sure to make mistakes but remember that it is only those who do nothing that can do nothing wrong. And also remember when you sometimes get the impression that everyone is picking on you in particular, that somewhere, sometime, every senior designer also had to learn from the beginning.

So do whatever you are asked cheerfully and as well as you

know how. Keep a smile ready and keep your eyes and ears open to all that is going on in your busy workroom. For this way lies success and, fortunately, in our world of flowers, there is still plenty of room at the top.

2 Wires and general equipment

Wires are used to support and control flower stems and also to give a design more stability than it would have if everything were left to go its own way.

This does not mean that heavy wires must always be used so that the flowers become so rigid that they lose all their natural appeal. It is most important that a design never looks 'manufactured'. Nevertheless, since bouquets and funeral tributes are usually subjected to a certain amount of handling, the competent florist will choose the correct gauge of wire to give the design just the right amount of support – no more and no less.

Only practice and experience will help you to know instinctively which wire is needed, but the first step towards this ideal situation is a thorough understanding of the wires that are in general use.

They are usually bought in bundles of one gauge and length weighing about 2.5 kg. Most are labelled with the metric size only though some have both metric and the standard wire gauge sizing (swg) while some are still only identified by swg or bwg (British wire gauge). This means that the florist must know both types of gauge.

2.5 kg

FLORIST WIRE
BLUE ANNEALED

0.70 x 180mm BWG 22 x 7"

1 *Typical BWG label*

9

Gauges are indicated from the largest to the finest wire and lengths from the shortest to the longest.

1.25 mm (18 swg)	0.38 mm (28 swg)
1.00 mm (19 swg)	0.32 mm (30 swg)
0.90 mm (20 swg)	0.28 mm (32 swg)
0.70 mm (22 swg)	0.24 mm (34 swg)
0.56 mm (24 swg)	0.20 mm (36 swg)
0.46 mm (26 swg)	

Wire is also available on reels or bobbins and has a variety of uses in the workroom from binding moss to wire frames (where these are still used for funeral tributes) to binding bouquets.

Wire storage   Most florists store their wires in heavy-based containers which must be tall enough to support the bundles without being easily knocked over. On no account store them in glass jars for if one should be accidentally shattered the result is chaos. Picking up wires that have been accidentally scattered all over the floor is a tedious job and if mixed with broken glass as well this is one facet of experience one can well do without.

Each wire container should be clearly labelled with the number of the gauge and on no account should they be mixed. *Lengths* of the same gauge could possibly be mixed although it is far more professional to keep everything separate.

Wires should be kept as dry as possible. The greencoated type are unaffected by water, but the blue annealed ones still tend to rust, which makes both hands and flower material dirty.

String is also a basic part of workroom equipment. It is used for binding funeral sheaves and sometimes for binding moss on to funeral frames. Some florists use ordinary brown string, while others prefer the green-dyed twine, of which there are several varieties and thicknesses. Plastic tape is also used.

Raffia or string is used for binding presentation bouquets. For very delicate or brittle stems that are unwired bind with **wool**. This will stretch and grip the stems without cutting them.

Florists' tape is a finishing tape for sealing the stem ends or base of a flower after being wired for inclusion in bouquets, button-holes or corsages. It comes in many colours, including several greens, brown, black, scarlet and pastel tints. The greens are the most popular as they help to maintain the natural look of a design. Brown is sometimes used for dried designs. This tape should not be stored anywhere near a radiator; it needs to be kept cool otherwise it tends to become sticky.

Flower preservative is in powder form in small sachets. There are several makes, and directions for use are printed on the sachet. It mixes into a solution that keeps the flower water germ-free and which also feeds the cut flower. It has been proved beyond all doubt that fresh flowers conditioned in a solution of flower preservative will last far longer than those just stood in plain water. It is logical, also, to soak the floral foam in the same solution.

Floral foam is a material which, after being thoroughly soaked, forms a base into which flower and foliage stems are driven to make an arrangement. It is also a vital ingredient of most modern funeral tributes. There is a number of recognised brand names and the florist uses whichever is found in practice to be the most satisfactory for his or her particular work. It comes in cartons of large bricks, squares or rounds. When dry, it is almost weightless. It soaks up the water quickly and should always be cut after being soaked, never when dry. Take care not to let pieces clog the drain.

Dry foam is used almost exclusively for fabric and dried designs. It is usually brown, is very light in weight and should never be put in water. Unlike the green foam, it can be cut dry as it has a completely different consistency.

Prongs or **frogs**, as they are sometimes called, are small green plastic supports on which the foam is impaled.

Oasis-Fix is an oil-based adhesive used continuously in the workroom. The prongs can be stuck to the container with fix, ribbons may be secured in place with it; candle-cups are attached with its help. Its uses are manifold and, fortunately, it is one of the few items that is not expensive. A roll will last some time if carefully used. It will never dry completely hard; it is not a glue. It will stick to any surface provided it is completely dry, and once attached, it tolerates being under water. As it is oil-based it may leave a stain on wood so first mask the base with tape, then put the small piece of 'Fix' on the tape so that it peels off cleanly. Plastic, glass or ceramic can easily be cleaned with white spirit. **Oasis-Fix** is a brand-name and so far as we know there is no other similar product that does exactly the same thing.

Candle-cups are shallow containers with a very short 'stem' that fits into a smaller container. They are available in several sizes, in white, black, silver or gold. Very few of the stems fit precisely, so they should be packed around with *Oasis-Fix*.

Other general equipment in a flower shop includes cards, envelopes, ribbons, wrapping paper, corsage boxes, pins, plastic saucers (for basket arrangements and special designs) candles and probably many different shapes and sizes of containers.

Ribbons really belong in a special category of their own for they form one of the most glamorous facets of the florist's equipment. They are also one of the most expensive. But whatever the quantity or variety of ribbons kept in stock, it must always be in good order. If you are asked to cut a length of ribbon, cut it neatly and as precisely to the right length as possible. It is very annoying for your employer to see the odd chunk of ribbon being cut off and trampled underfoot. It is also a waste of time and ribbon if it has been cut carelessly so that the next person has to cut yet another piece away to neaten the end. Ribbon should always be cut to a sharp slope, not in a 'fish-tail'.

Wrapping paper, particularly if it is printed, is another very costly item. But a good paper, with a striking design, will, like shop colours and a logo, do a great deal for public relations. When you wrap flowers, tear the paper carefully, so that you get a neat and not a jagged edge. Some shops are using cellophane almost exclusively. This is particularly attractive for gift-wrap, as combined with ribbon, it has a very festive appearance.

As a student-florist you may possibly be given the job of keeping the equipment in order and you will be surprised at what a full-time job it can be. Greetings cards and care cards, for example there should always be several types of greetings cards available for general gifts. Then there are birthdays, wedding anniversaries, St Valentine's Day (big business, this!), plus Easter, Mothers' Day and, of course, Christmas. All the relevant cards must be on show – and, of course, the reverse. Nothing is more depressing than seeing a group of Christmas greetings cards left around till New Year.

There are special cards for sympathy and funeral tributes; these are generally kept in another display case, with cellophane envelopes handy, for all cards fixed to funeral tributes should be covered to protect them from the weather.

Care cards apply to cut flowers, arrangements and plants. These also should be displayed according to the appropriate season, so that they are immediately on hand for the florist to include in the envelope with the greetings card.

Most people rise to the challenge of responsibility. Taking care of the dry goods supplies could well be one of the student-florist's first jobs. As well as all the items previously listed, supplies of pins, paper clips, staples, order pads, pens, rough paper (what in America is known as scratch paper), dry dusters, not forgetting basic refreshment such as tea, coffee and sugar, should never run out!

None of this appears in the shop by magic and things run far more smoothly if one person is responsible for keeping the score, so to speak. It could be that your shop already uses a requisition list, but if not, this is an area which you could easily take care of. Make a list of all the items in use in the shop. How frequently these are re-ordered depends, obviously, on how quickly stocks are used, but also on how much storage space is available. Generally, most principals prefer to buy as much at one time as possible. It minimises time spent either on the telephone or in writing letters, fewer cheques have to be written and consequently, there is less filing to be done. The only pitfall in having ample supplies is that one tends to think that the supply is inexhaustible and then, suddenly, one is out of some vital item.

Since wires and ribbons are probably two of the items most quickly used up, it is best to keep separate order sheets for these two. The rest can possibly go on one sheet; thus, a requisition list would look something like this:

Wire list

Gauge and length	Bundles	Reels	Date taken	Bundles left	Reels left
1.25 × 460 (18 × 18)	4			3	
.90 × 260 (20 × 10)	8			6	
.28 silver (32)		12			12

NOTE   The gauge is always stated first, the length second. The buyer has only to check the last two columns to know what wires remain 'on the shelf'. It is then his responsibility to order accordingly.

In this example, no silver reel wire was absorbed into general use, so the stock remains static.

Ribbon list
It is best to record the widths and to staple a small piece of the actual ribbon to the list. Colour numbers are also useful, but the buyer may not be able to carry the colour of a particular number in his or her head. Should this number be out of stock it may be necessary to buy the next best and a pattern here would be very useful.

Some ribbon colours are far more in use than others. They will also vary with the seasons; for example, in Springtime lemon, blue, mauve and light green are always in use for bouquets and gift-wrap, ie bouquets of cut flowers. Later in the year more brown and orange are needed, with plenty of scarlet and dark green for Christmas. Therefore ribbons, as well as greetings cards, can be displayed or stored according to the season. Try not to have two reels of the same colour 'on the go' as this may confuse the stock check. Keep satin and polypropylene ribbons in separate containers and it also helps to keep colours in groups; for example, all the various greens on one row of the ribbon bank. This can either be fixed to the wall or be portable. In a busy shop, both types are useful.

3 Basic design

It is fascinating to look in a dictionary and find the various meanings of the word *design*. Two of the most forceful are 'mental plan' and 'scheme of attack'. It goes on to say 'to contrive, to plan, to intend'. Obviously most appropriate, for we need all of this in the flower shop as well as in our private lives. Without plan or intention, it is doubtful if any of us would ever get out of bed in the morning, let alone make a flower design!

As florists, however, we are simply concerned with the bare meaning of the word design which implies, in general, that everything that comes from the florist's workroom needs a good deal of thought.

And so it does. Fortunately, however, the same sets of rules apply almost consistently, regardless of what you are making. For example, although a facing arrangment in a vase looks very little like a bridal bouquet, yet it should be constructed according to the same basic formula.

There is a world of difference in size and appearance between a lapel spray, sometimes called a corsage, and a funeral sheaf. Yet if you understand the guidelines for the one design, you should be able to make the other, still applying the same basic principles.

Think of the five-finger exercise on the piano; it is incredible how much real music an accomplished musician can produce using only those five notes. And, at most, the scale, which is a simple progression of the eight notes of the octave, is all he has in the way of raw material for making music.

The florist is working with something far more tangible: with flowers and foliage in a multitude of shapes, sizes and colours, offering an almost infinite variety of possibilities. But unless these raw materials are understood and the basic principles of design are respected, a confusing muddle may emerge, rather like when a very young child amuses himself at the piano keyboard.

Primarily, there are two aspects of design with flowers; the visual and the technical. The visual is that which we see. The technical is the method of work which we follow to achieve the visual.

The Technical

Any good design, be it a flower arrangement or a cathedral, needs reliable foundations. The choice of a suitable container or base is of paramount importance. It should be the right size for the design. So what is the right size? Here the technical impinges on the visual. It should be large enough to make a significant base for the flowers yet not so large that it dwarfs the material.

1 Stability is vital to good design. Having decided on the container, it must be prepared so that the arrangement stays firm, even in transit. Some of the commercial containers are manufactured with a rim inside which supports the block of soaked foam. But this will not give total stability so it is usually advisable to secure the block with either *Oasis-tape* or *Sellotape*. The container and your hands must be dry otherwise the tape will not stick. *Sellotape* is very reliable provided you use it generously: it stretches slightly, so pull very hard and bring it right around the bowl so that it sticks to itself and not just to the container. Figure 2.

2 *Making a base stable*

Should the tape bite into the foam, place a small piece of stem under it to act as a cushion. This is not usually necessary when making small arrangements, but for really large ones, such as pedestals and church designs, it is vital.

Figure 3 illustrates the main points of design from the technical point of view. Figures 4 and 5 indicate the various options for shape and outline.

2 Vertical This will be your initial guide line. It will probably be the first flower or piece of foliage to be put in place and should mark the highest point in the outline.

3 Laterals These will initially establish the width of the design. Other lines will echo both the vertical and the lateral, thus building up a complete design.

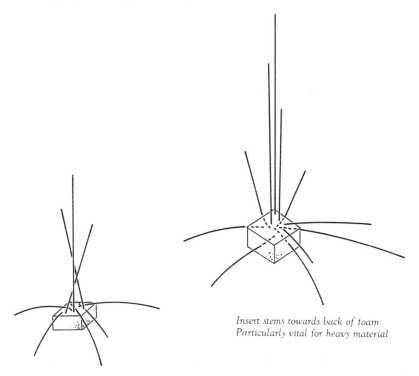

Insert stems towards back of foam. Particularly vital for heavy material

Flowers in same position but stems wrongly placed

3 *Main points of design*

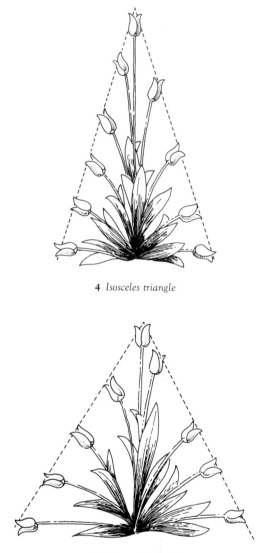

4 *Isosceles triangle*

5 *Equilateral triangle*

4 Point of origin The place where all stems *appear* to meet.
Figure 6. Obviously they cannot all be driven into the same place
on the foam, but they should all *seem* to flow into and away from a
central 'heart'. This concept is very important both from the
technical and the visual point of view. It requires constant

6 *The place where all stems appear to meet*

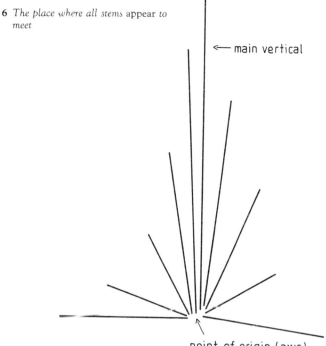

← main vertical

point of origin (axis)

vigilance and a great deal of practice. A flower may be in exactly the right place in an arrangement, but the angle of the stem may be wrong, thus sounding a sour note in the design.

5 **Balance** is controlled by placing the material properly; far easier said than done! When making a facing design, insert the majority of stems as far back in the foam block as possible, even to the extent of leaving the front bit completely unused. This will not mean that your facing design is completely flat both at the back and the front, for if only a few flowers are set towards the front these will ensure a pleasing profile.

The visual
The visual aspect of any design involves *Shape, Outline, Balance, Colour* and *Texture*. These are the main attributes or ingredients of good design in any field you care to mention.

1 **Shape** implies the general impression of the design as a whole. Relative to a container arrangement, this not only includes the flowers and foliage, but also the container. Shape can also be sub-divided into *profile* and *depth*, both of which are particularly valid when the design is viewed from several angles; for example, a bridal bouquet, a facing design in, perhaps, a hotel foyer or other similar situation, or even a lapel spray, which is seen from both left and right, as well as from the front.

2 **Outline** suggests definition of shape; the instant visual registration of height and width.

3 **Balance** in the visual sense is the natural outcome of good design. The complete picture, flowers and container, should give pleasure; the arrangement should be right for the environment: in balance that is, with the surroundings. Colour, shape and size of material will be exploited to advantage, so that the arrangement blends with the container and does not seem to be just perched on top of it. Balance, also, must include a well-defined 'heart' or axis. Some people prefer to call this the focal point. However, in reality, the complete design, and not simply the centre of it, should be the focus of interest.

4 **Colour** is one of the most important tools or ingredients of design. However, all people see colour so differently that it is foolhardy to pontificate and lay down hard and fast rules as to its use, whether in floristry, interior decorating or, indeed in any other area. Guidelines can, however, be gently indicated, sugges-tions made, examples demonstrated, but we must all recognise that colour appreciation and understanding is still very much a personal matter.

The colour wheel is a formalised means of indicating the relationship of one colour to another. Even though florists cannot mix colours as on an artist's palette, the colour wheel can be a great help when planning designs or when used to check an arrangement that is not as effective as was hoped.

The wheel diagram has been left blank so that colour can be added, which will help in remembering the basics. For example, the three primary colours are indicated by the largest 'petals' on the wheel; red, yellow and blue. None of these three can be made by mixing other colours; hence the adjective 'primary'.

Secondary colour is produced by mixing two primary colours together. These could, of course, be mixed in precise fifty-fifty proportions, thus resulting in an exact secondary colour, midway

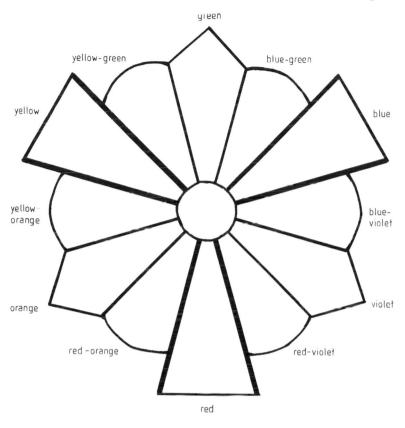

green

yellow-green   blue-green

yellow   blue

yellow-orange   blue-violet

orange   violet

red-orange   red-violet

red

7 *Colour wheel*

between the two primary colours.

Alternatively, they could be mixed in varying proportions with emphasis towards one primary colour or the other. For example, orange is the product of mixing red and yellow in equal proportions. But a red-orange contains more red, while a yellow-orange contains more yellow than red. This can be coloured in on the wheel after the primary colours have been completed.

A colour harmony check can easily be constructed by tracing the shapes shown on pages 24 to 26 on to separate sheets of heavy cartridge paper or thin card, and cutting them out, leaving the rest of the sheet blank. Place the sheet over the wheel, in any position you wish. The colours showing through the space or spaces will give you the colour harmony wanted.

Monochromatic harmony does not pose any real problem for, as the name implies, it means using only one basic colour, although to avoid visual boredom it is possible to use this one colour in varying intensities. For example, an arrangement of delphiniums, from very deep to pale blue, or spray carnations, red to palest pink. In fact, flowers need not all be the same kind, for delphiniums could be mixed with iris or campanula; spray carnations with roses and/or sweet peas, provided only one basic colour is used.

A complementary harmony is produced by using colours opposite on the colour wheel. However, it is usually not very satisfactory to make an arrangement with exactly the same number of flowers of each colour, for this can produce visual boredom. Far more emphasis and interest can be achieved by using more of one colour with, perhaps, paler or darker tints of the same basic colours. Remember, also, that you do not necessarily have to start with a primary colour. The check sheet can be placed in any position you wish and it is fun to move it around to see what results emerge.

Analogous harmony must contain only one primary colour with the addition of other tints either one side or even both sides of that primary colour. Be very careful not to stray over into another primary colour and this is one good reason why the spaces on your check sheets must be cut out very precisely.

Triadic harmony produces an interesting, lively or appealing design, according to the intensity and quantity of colours used. But success depends not only on using the right quantity of each colour, but also on masterly grouping and placement of material.

This, then, in very simple terms, is the theory of colour which we, the florists, have to try to translate into living material. But it is possible to apply the theory of colour only so far; for example, one adds white to a paint colour for a paler effect. Yet to introduce white flowers into a design may have the reverse effect of intensifying, by contrast, the very colour you were hoping to dilute. However, the theory of colour as applied to floristry keeps one constantly alert to the power and influence of colour. This is particularly vital when designing arrangements for hospital for it must always be remembered that people who are ill are especially vulnerable.

However, please do not let all these headings and definitions daunt you. There will only be a certain number of different flowers and foliages available at any given time, but, like the notes of the octave, it is how they are used that adds up to impact and success.

The following table is a rough guide to the amount of colour, in terms of units, that can be used in relation to another colour. This is worked out on the power of impact of any given colour relative to grey. It also must apply to flowers of a similar size.

Yellow – 3 units
Red – 6 units
Blue – 8 units
Orange – 4 units
Violet – 9 units
Green – 6 units

From this it is easy to see which are the most outgoing colours. In fact, colour symbolism is equally absorbing.

Yellow signifies light and knowledge
Red signifies power
Blue signifies faith and meekness
Orange signifies pride and self-respect
Violet signifies piety
Green signifies sympathy and compassion
White signifies purity and the essence of light

How much of the above is fact and how much is fable remains to be seen. All the same, there are colour harmonies in flowers that are soothing, others are exhilarating while some, unfortunately less successful, strike the beholder as just boring.

5   **Texture** is yet another absorbing facet of design in floristry. Texture can readily be understood in relation to fabrics. For example, a piece of rough tweed and a piece of silk, both the same size and dyed to the identical tint, yet the visual effect as well as the feel of the material, is completely different.

Texture variations in flowers and foliage are, possibly, not quite so dramatic, yet compare an arum lily with a carnation, a tulip with a rose; smooth silvery iris foliage with bright green crinkly pittosporum leaves, or holly foliage with eucalyptus populus.

So many factors add up to good design. Analyse for yourself

why a particular thing appeals, not necessarily a flower arrangement. The impact, or not, of a shop window or an individual item displayed may catch your eye; what is it that makes you stop in your tracks? Try to make time to visit art galleries and exhibitions of ceramics and jewellery, even look objectively at some of the buildings in your town. Everything is a product, for better or worse, of someone's plan of design. Alert yourself to other art forms so that, in time, it will be possible to feed back impressions into your own designs.

Shapes for colour harmony check
Monochromatic colour harmony   One colour only is used, but is varied by using materials in different levels of intensity but all related to the basic colour.

Complementary colour harmony   Colours directly opposite each other on the colour wheel.

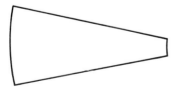 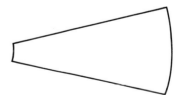

Analogous colour harmony Several neighbouring colours on any particular section of the circle, but containing only ONE primary colour.

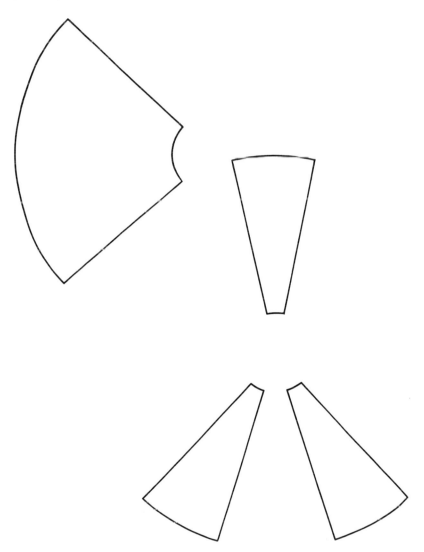

Split complementary colour harmony Incorporates two colours opposite the basic colour and either side of the true complimentary.

Triadic colour harmony   The use of colours equidistant on the colour wheel. A pleasing result is reached by using the colours in varying levels of intensity and in uneven quantities of material.

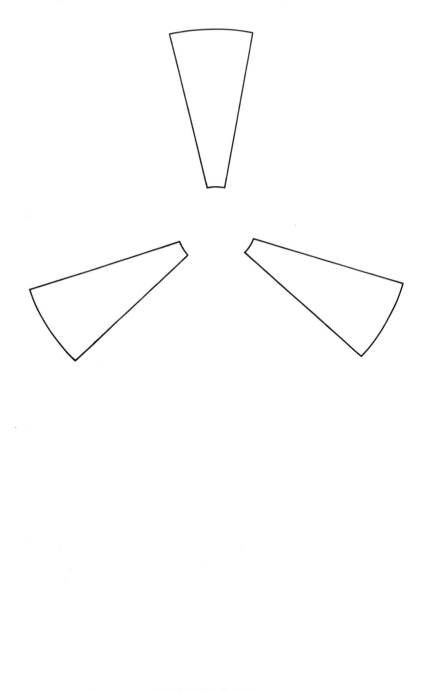

4 Wiring methods

Why do we wire flowers? Some people take the view that it is a great shame to impale them on wire and thus cause them to appear unnatural. They could not be more right. It is not only a shame, it is clumsy and stupid to make any flower look stiff and unnatural. Yet it is equally sad to allow beautiful blooms to be bent and shattered for want of a little discreet support and control.

Discreet is the operative word, for modern flower design dictates that everything shall appear as natural as possible and the over-contrived look is not only down-market but decidedly old-fashioned.

This is why it is vital that exactly the right gauge of wire is selected and that the wire, if applied outside the stem, is always kept as close to the stem as possible. So how do we make these decisions? Actually, 50% of the decision is made for the florist by the flowers themselves; their form, their size and the type of stem. All these factors will indicate clues as to which wiring method is appropriate, while other points will guide the decision as to which gauge is required; for example, the strength of the stem, the weight of the flower, what type of design the wired material is intended for and also if it is destined for a warm atmosphere, open-air or wherever: all these points should be evaluated.

Taping   This plays an important role in preparing bridal design flowers. First, the objective; why do we bother to tape, for before this material was available, the flower stems were masked with copious quantities of asparagus fern. The flowers themselves, regardless of form or weight, were usually wired on wire 1.25 or 1.00 (18 or 19). Not only that, all was inserted into a moss ball. One can just imagine the weight of a bridal bouquet!

Wired stems, however short and fine, are now finished with tape which helps seal the stem and therefore limits any further dehydration. There is a number of different types of tape and florists have their own favourite brands. It is available in numerous colours and when it first came on the market it was thought very stylish to match the tape tint to the flower. Thus, a pink bouquet would be finished with pink tape, a blue one with blue, and so on. But this looked very contrived and most people prefer green for fresh material and brown for dried flowers and foliage. White may be appropriate for some occasions; for example, a bride cake top or for finishing a prayerbook spray. The decision must rest with the designer.

Tape splitting   Except for flowers with large and/or very juicy stems, halving the tape width results in a much finer finish. This can, of course, be done with sharp large-bladed scissors. There are also several varieties of tape splitter available, the basis being a firm stand and spool to hold the reel of tape, which is then guided over a blade.

Mount wire   This means the addition of another (sometimes stronger) wire to the wired flower. It is necessary when preparing units for bridal designs and also for some funeral designs. The mount wire enables the florist to angle the flower or unit and thus control the shape of the design. In essence, therefore, the first wire is for *support*, the mount wire is for *control*.

There are a few exceptions to this technique. Foliage for edging a funeral tribute is usually mounted but not wired. A flower on a short strong stem may not require a support wire but might need to be mounted for quick insertion into the base.

Flower form groups
As a general guide to wiring decisions, flowers can be divided roughly into three groups.
1 Those with a strong calyx, such as rose and carnation.
2 Flowers with a small calyx in relation to the size of the bloom, eg chrysanthemum, dahlia.
3 Flowers with little or no calyx, such as tulip, iris, hyacinth, orchid.

Stem texture groups
Stems, also, fall into three main categories.
1 Woody stems like chrysanthemum, rose.

2 Hollow stems as in daffodil, zinnia, cornflower.
3 Semi-hollow stems, eg tulip, iris.

The word *hollow* is applied as the opposite to *woody*, for not all stems in category 3 have tube-like formation. Rather they are fleshy yet will accept the internal wiring method.

External wiring foliage
Stitch method   With the underside of the leaf towards you, insert silver wire .32 (30) at an angle very neatly across the central vein about two-thirds of the way up the leaf or one-third down from the tip. Figure 8.

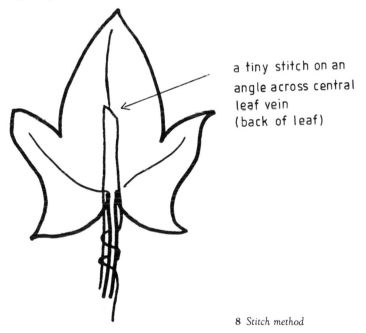

a tiny stitch on an
angle across central
leaf vein
(back of leaf)

8 *Stitch method*

Then grasp the leaf firmly between finger and thumb at the point where the wire punctures it. This prevents the wire from moving and possibly making the two tiny holes larger. Also the holes are less likely to tear if they are not directly in line.

Draw the two legs of wire down parallel with one another each side of the central vein. Wind one end of wire round the other and around the leaf stem twice.

Rose leaves Select two leaves the same size, lay them one on top of the other and stitch through the two together as indicated above. Stitch method is valid for most foliage, the exception being heavy-textured leaves such as stephanotis, tradescantia and zebrina; in fact, any thick fleshy leaves are best supported by the *Sellotape* method as follows:

First make sure that your hand, the foliage and workbench are completely dry. Double the silver .32 (30) wire, lay it in line with the central vein and fix with a strip of *Sellotape*. If the leaf is very long, eg chlorophytum, it will be necessary to add a second wire to continue the support. Add a second strip of *Sellotape* to broad leaves, eg scindapsus, philodendron, across the central vein for added support.

When the design is sprayed will the *Sellotape* hold? It not only tolerates spraying, but should not peel off even if the foliage is submerged in water for a short time. If the tape refuses to adhere, check the brand, for some varieties are much stronger than others.

Category 1 External wiring A carnation is probably the easiest flower on which to begin wiring practice. It has a good solid calyx and the bloom is not easily shattered.

Method Take the wire in your right hand, the flower in the left, holding it just under the flower head. Hold the wire parallel to the flower stem with the point aimed at the underneath of the calyx. Keeping the wire parallel to the stem insert the tip firmly into the calyx. Drive it well in until you feel a slight check as the wire comes into contact with the seed pod within the bloom. You then know that you have reached target and the long end of wire can be gently persuaded round and down the stem at an angle of about 45 degrees, see figure 9. Do not twist too much otherwise it may look like a corkscrew. Notice that the size of wire has not been mentioned for I have no idea what type of carnation you are wiring. It may be a very strong one, with a very firm stem and you need to ensure that the head is not snapped off in handling, for possibly it is intended for a funeral spray. On the other hand, the flower may have a rather whippy stem. In the first instance, my preference would be to use a green .56 or, at most .70 (24 or 22), for only the bloom is at risk. But the second flower with a weak

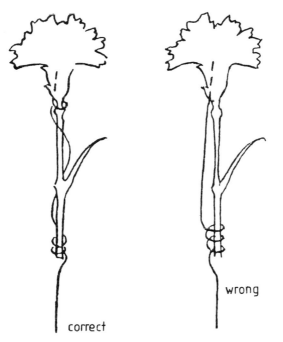

wrong

correct

9 *External wiring method*

stem will require stronger support and probably wire .70 or .90 (22 or 20) would be necessary.

One other point before progressing to the next category; left-handed people will obviously work the reverse way from the right-handed ones. This applies not only to wiring, but also to taping.

Category 2 Internal wiring From the point of view of design this is the nicest group of all for the wires can be inserted inside the stem, thus being completely invisible.

Hook method The wire may be driven upwards right into the flower and beyond, see figure 10. Make a small hook and then retract the wire so that the hook rests within the flower. Take care not to retract it too far otherwise the wire may puncture the flower fabric.

Alternatively, make the small hook first, then insert the other end of the wire down through the flower into the stem until the hook is resting within the bloom. Which of these two methods

10 *Internal hook method*

you use can sometimes be a matter of preference; at other times the form of the flower and stem will make the decision for you.

Probably the majority of wiring will be by the internal hook method; but there are exceptions. Flowers with an open centre, for example, single spray chrysanthemum and gerbera, should not be hooked for this will show, however carefully it is done. To support a gerbera on a long stem, drive a straight wire into the centre of the flower and down through the stem. Gently press the tip of the wire right into the middle of the bloom until it is completely out of sight.

It is unlikely, however, that this method will suit a single spray chrysanthemum as usually the stem is so hollow that the wire would just drop through. Here are two possible uses for a wired spray chrysanthemum, single variety only.

1 It might be on maximum stem-length for insertion into a bridal posy or presentation bouquet, that is about 10 cm long.

2 On a very short stem for a solid-based funeral tribute.

EXAMPLE 1   Insert the wire right up to the flower head. Place your finger on the centre of the flower: if the wire pricks it, you know you have gone too far. You have to be really careful about this, for once the flower is bound into the design it is impossible to push the wire back out of sight or to cut it off. This first wire will support your flower but it has no anchorage, so insert a second wire as far up the stem as possible (it may only be for about 2 cm but this will be sufficient to block the stem and prevent the first wire from moving. Figure 11 (a). You will, of course, tape the end of the stem which fixes the wires even more.

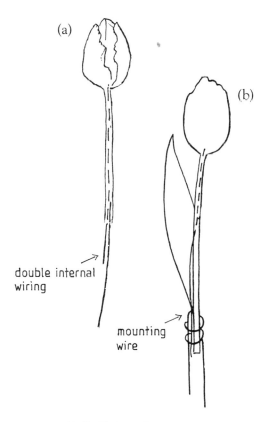

11 *Double internal wiring*

EXAMPLE 2   The short-stemmed open-centred (single) flower can be wired externally in the same way as wiring the carnation. Alternatively, you have more control by holding the flower upside down between finger and thumb, so that the head does not drop off, and by driving the wire carefully through the calyx, pinching it down parallel with the stem, twisting once around itself and the flower stem, so that the flower is wired on a double leg. This is an expedient, but is by no means ideal since it punctures the material twice. In other words, only adopt this method when no other will work to your satisfaction, see figure 12.

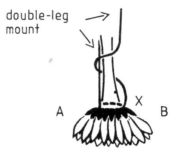

12 *Driving wire through calyx*

Category 3 This is a combination of methods 1 and 2, that is, both external and internal wiring on one stem. Where a leaf joins the stem there is usually a joint called a *node*, for instance, a tulip, iris, and carnation stem. It is not generally possible to drive a wire through this node. Therefore the wire should be inserted above the first node and be driven inside the stem into the flower. The piece of wire outside the stem is then wound around and down the stem as for category 1. Figure 11 (b).

Rose pinning
This is a way of keeping a bud rose from opening in very warm weather.

Method Cut some silver wire .32 or .38 (30 or 28) into short lengths of not more than 3 cm. Double them to make small hairpins. *Before* the roses are conditioned carefully pin each sepal to the bud, inserting the pin vertically, so that the five (one into each sepal) are less noticeable than if they are inserted horizontally, pointing, so to speak, east-west rather than north-south. Rose pinning should only be used for bouquets or other made-up work and not for roses as cut flowers. Some varieties hold their shape longer than others; so it is not necessary to pin every rose in a design, but only the ones that you want to stay pointed and bud-shaped.

If you attempt to pin after the roses have taken up water the sepals will resist and may break.

Lily-of-the-valley and stephanotis should also be wired before being conditioned. With silver reel wire .20 or .24 (36 or 34) carefully wind between the florets, upwards to the tip, leaving at least 5 cm of spare wire loose below the first floret. Very carefully wind the wire around the tiny fragile stem of the topmost floret, then cut the wire off as close to the floret as you dare. Condition the flowers with their stems in shallow water until they are required, figure 13.

13 *External wiring of fragile stems*

To mount lily-of-the-valley Insert wire .56 (24) into each stem, driving it as far up as possible. Hold a leaf against the stem and secure it with the spare silver wire left at the base of the flower head. Wind it down the stem and on to the mount wire, thus securing it. Tape with full width tape. Lay each prepared flower on a damp towel. Do not stand the mount wire in a block of foam or in a container. For although this looks very professional, the delicate (and expensive) flowers will be at risk from draughts. Also by standing them perpendicular the water may drain down from the flower head and diminish its lasting quality.

Stephanotis This should be wired without previously conditioning. Generally the florets are packed in polythene envelopes
containing 25 to 30 florets and buds. Cut each stem to about 2 cm
and using internal hook method, drive a silver wire .46 (26)
upwards through the stem and into the flower. If the wire refuses,
cut a fraction off the stem and try again. Obviously it is not
possible to make a hook in the tight buds, so having inserted one
wire right into the bud, add a second one into the stem (the same
method as for a spray chrysanthemum). Tape each flower as soon
as it is wired and, if possible, build them into units as well. The
flowers should then be packed either in a polythene bag or a box,
well sprayed and stored in a cool place till required. Good quality
stephanotis will last for several days if kept completely free from
draught.

Freesia florets These bell-shaped flowers can be wired
individually by the hook method. However, the flower fabric is
less durable than stephanotis or hyacinth, for the flowers
dehydrate fairly rapidly. All the same, freesia is a very popular
flower for lapel sprays and head-dresses.

Method 1 Tape the top 1 cm of a silver wire .38 or .46 (28 or 26)
using pale green, half width. Make the hook and insert the wire
down through the floret till the taped hook is resting within.

Method 2 Make the hook and then catch a tiny piece of cotton
wool (cotton) on it. Dip it into clean water and then insert wire
into the floret as above.

   The tape 'padding' on the hook will help protect the fabric of
the flower as you overtape it, while obviously the damp cotton
wool will do this even more efficiently. Method 1 is far quicker
since the taped 'stamens' can be prepared in advance and stored in
a clean jar with a lid.

Method 3 Carefully tape the base of the floret. With silver wire
.38 (28) support the flower loop method, that is, make a loop in
the wire, so that one end is longer than the other. Lay the loop on
the material (in this instance the freesia floret protected with tape).
Bind the longer end of wire twice around the flower and itself and
tape over.

   Good-quality freesia on the stem rarely needs much support,
but it is sometimes prudent to wire the first open flower. Should

the whole flower head need support, use the same method as for lily-of-the-valley.

Orchids Some varieties are relatively heavy, both in texture and actual weight. Others are extremely delicate and must be wired accordingly. Try to wire the flower internally. Cattleya, cymbidium and cyprepedium orchids will usually tolerate this but take care as you insert the wire up through the flower. A fresh orchid will be springy and the lip will usually bounce back into place once the hook is safely hidden deep in the flower. A .56 (24) wire should be sufficient to support the bloom but, because of the weight of the stem, it may be necessary to insert another wire into the stem: perhaps a second one the same weight or a size larger, depending on how the flower is being used.

Vanda, phalaenopsis and odontoglossum varieties are more delicate and should be wired with extreme care. One method is to tape a wire, silver .38 or .46 (28 or 26), double it and gently place it across the centre of the flower bringing the two legs parallel with the stem. Alternatively, insert a silver .32 or .38 (30 or 28) into the stem just under the back petal. Twist it around the stem and tape (external wiring method). Most Singapore orchids can be wired by this method as the stems are usually too curved just behind the flower for internal wiring.

Roses On very short stems, for inclusion in corsages, headdresses, etc, it is usually possible to wire internally, in spite of the rose having a semi-woody stem. Hook method is appropriate for orange and red roses, but for paler tints and, of course, white roses, support them with the two-wire method. That is, one wire driven straight through the stem into the flower head; a second one inserted a little way into the stem. It is risky to use the hook method as it may damage the flower fabric and show bruising after several hours.

Roses on longer stems for insertion in bouquets and posies usually have to be wired externally. Tape the wire to within 1 cm of the tip. Insert this tip into the calyx and gently bind the taped wire around the stem. If you use green wires, check whether these, or an ordinary one taped, is the more visible. The green wires generally show rather darkly against the green rose stem.

It is a matter for debate whether these stems should be cut short and replaced with wires, for this was the technique in the days when matching tape was used. Every bloom was beheaded to a uniform stem length, which, together with the matching tape, resulted in usually a very artificial-looking design. It now seems more professional to present the flower as naturally as possible and that means, not only delicate wiring, but leaving as much stem as possible.

There can never be famous last words on methods of wiring. Techniques vary from one country to another, priorities are different and designers all over the world are forever experimenting with different materials. If in doubt as to the wiring method required, or the size of wire appropriate, try first with a lightweight wire. You can always add another, or even change it for a heavier gauge. Some flowers, in fact, will not tolerate the weight of wire needed to support them. Roses are a case in point. The flower itself needs a light wire which is nothing like strong enough for building into a design. Therefore more wire must be added to the stem to counterbalance the weight of the flower.

Unit assembly
This means taping already-wired and taped material to a 'backbone' or support wire so that it can be included in a design. Figure 14. Units vary considerably in size and weight, but for bouquets, no one support wire should be expected to carry too much weight. Therefore, as an extension of the concept discussed in the previous paragraph, it is sometimes necessary to build more support wires on to a unit so that the weight of the material is carried through the tying point down to the handle.

It is astonishing how tolerant most flower material is to being removed from the plant, wired and taped and assembled into designs. Always be alert to putting new material on trial. First condition it, then wire and tape and leave it exposed for several hours. If it is still crisp, you can most likely rely on it for your design.

19 swg
1·00 mm

24 swg
0·56 mm

14 *Unit assembly*

5 Arrangements

Objectives

In chapter 3 the basics of good design are discussed. So what are our objectives when making flower arrangements on a commercial basis? Certainly it is completely different from arranging flowers at home. Then we have only ourselves to please, and if by chance a flower slips out of position, someone is usually handy to put it right.

Most designs either for shop display or for a client have to be made to fit in with someone else's taste. And very likely it must be made within the confines of a specific price. Also, and this is really vital, the arrangement must be firm enough in the container to tolerate being transported from shop to delivery address. If several points have been repeated here and elsewhere, it is because they are so important that they should be repeated, one might even add, three times a day after meals. The stability of an arrangement can never be overemphasised.

The first objective of a commercial flower design of any kind is to make an impact, that is, that its effect on the beholder is both pleasing and positive. The instant feed-back should be one of both pleasure and satisfaction. A high ideal, but one well-worth aiming for.

The diagram on the facing page indicates some of the aspects of impact: the component parts, one might call them.

Definitions of some terms in general use in floristry

Impact　Immediate visual impression; therefore commercially speaking, for TOTAL customer satisfaction, this must be 100%

Line　Conveys the design intent of outline, shape and flow

Grouping and repetition　An extension of line. Material placed so as to give emphasis and strength to design

Rhythm flow　Material placed so that it gives maximum visual movement to the design

Recession　Material placed usually towards the centre of the design so that colour lines are continuous, so that each flower is

seen to its best advantage and so that the centre of the design has
visual strength

Balance   Visual   This means that the design is comfortable and
pleasant to look at

Actual   This is a question of technique. The base
should be properly prepared and the material should be
correctly placed

Distinction   Use of material in an unusual way that lifts the design
from 'ordinary and satisfactory' to 'special and outstanding'.
Distinction does not rely on expensive or unusual material

Objectives

Customer satisfaction
Creative satisfaction
Financial satisfaction

IMPACT

Line	Grouping	Rhythm
Outline	Repetition	Flow
	Use of colour	Economy
	Recession	
	Distinction	
	Visual satisfaction =	

IMPACT

Equipment and planning

1 *The Container*   This seems basic and very obvious, but basic
equipment should first be assembled before flowers and foliage
are taken out of water. True, this is sometimes a 'chicken and egg'
situation, for one needs to know which flowers and foliage before
deciding on type and dimensions of the container

2 *Soaked foam* and the tackle for fixing it securely:
Oasis-fix
A *prong* or *frog*
Fixing tape
Kleenex tissues

3 A *sprayer* (mister)

4 A *few wires* may sometimes be needed

Preparing the container The quickest way to fix foam to the container is to impale it on a prong which must be fixed when the container is completely dry for although *Oasis-fix* tolerates water, it will never stick firmly unless the base of the prong, your hands and the container are absolutely dry. *Oasis-fix* never dries out completely but the longer it is left, the firmer it is. To give the foam block extra stability (for transportation) run a length of tape around it and round the bowl part of the container, pulling the tape very firmly and finally sticking it to itself, not just to the container. Never begin an arrangement until you are satisfied that the foam block is thoroughly stable, and this applies to all designs, from the smallest to the most opulent.

Highly-glazed ceramic containers, also glass, may sometimes reject the *Oasis-fix*, even though it is applied when all is quite dry. Fortunately the solution is simple. Fold a *Kleenex* tissue to the size of the foam block, set it in the container and stand the foam on top. Then tape in very firmly. The tissue will prevent the foam block from skidding on the glass or high glaze.

Decision *What size of foam block?* This must be determined by the size of design planned and also the size and weight of the flowers and foliage. The ideal is a piece large enough to support all the material properly, yet not so big that it takes too much time and material to mask it, for once a stem is inserted it makes a hole, so not only the size and weight of the flowers have to be evaluated, but also the diameter of the stems. A design containing gladioli and gerbera, for example, will require a much larger block of foam than a design of the same dimensions containing carnations and roses.

Masking the foam One of the quickest and most attractive ways of masking (for not a glimpse of the foam should be seen when the design is complete) is to pin a few pieces of fresh green moss on to the block here and there, but not to cover it completely, for there must still be space for the flower stems. Make the hairpins from short pieces of wire .56 (24) or .70 (22). Alternatively, insert some short foliage, preferably one with fairly broad leaves that will cover economically. More masking can be added when the design is finished, but it is quicker to do most of this before the flowers and decorative foliage are inserted.

Working method Assemble everything needed for the design, keeping flowers and decorative foliage in a container, not lying on the workbench. So far as possible, work with one type of flower at a time as this method speeds up the work, particularly when making large display designs. Imagine you are painting the arrangement. Use strong sweeping lines beginning finely at the edges (buds and paler flowers) becoming stronger and more emphatic towards the centre (open flowers and stronger colours). Also too many different colours and flower shapes may result in a confused effect. These are very rough guidelines and, of course, there are numerous exceptions, where rules are gloriously broken and the results magnificent.

Grouping material helps to emphasise the lines of the design. For example, if there are only two or three of one type of flower, set them in a group, for then they will make far more impact than being scattered around the design.

Economy is vital in the workroom. But this does not imply that you should be mean with material. This is false economy and nothing is worse than that for the firm's public image. Proper economy means respecting every flower for its design possibilities, using each piece of foliage to its best advantage, so that all the various ingredients of the design really work for you instead of being just rather expensive passengers.

General The number of arrangements produced in a workroom depends, obviously, on the type of business, but in any case the trend is ever upwards: gift arrangements for anniversaries, for hospitals, to say 'thank-you', and for dinner parties as well as Christmas, Easter and other festivals, plus, of course, for special banquets, wedding receptions, hotel contracts and so on. Although these designs will appear to be totally different in size, personality and content, they will all be constructed in line with the basic guidelines. These vary to a certain extent from country to country, but in British floristry, the facing design and the all-round arrangement (radial forms) are the foundations on which we base most of our work.

Every design should have a 'bone formation'. This applies not only to container work but also to bouquets and some types of funeral designs. This really means that instead of being confused with a mass of flowers, you actually can see the lines – the skeleton on which the design is made. This basic bone formation, therefore, is an important ingredient in the design – the plan.

Facing arrangements

Facing designs are generally intended to be placed against a background: a pillar, a wall or a mirror, or possibly in the corner of a room or hall. It is valid for any situation where it could be seen from most angles but not from the back. Other examples of facing designs include a corsage, pinned on the lapel or worn as a shoulder spray, a bouquet carried against the background of the bridal gown and a funeral spray.

Another useful point when preparing the container for any design is to use a rectangular foam block in a round-topped container and a round block in a square container. Then there will be space to add water conveniently. Also when working on a square block, work from one corner and not from the centre of one side of the rectangle. This will give you slightly more design space which may be vital to the actual balance of the design.

The bone formation of this is three main lines, the vertical and two laterals, though these need not be set at right angles to the vertical. Having partly masked the foam base, the first vertical should be placed well back in the foam and inserted as deeply and as straight as possible. Add two more verticals of different heights and as close to the first one as possible. This will give you a good firm emphatic main line.

The left and right lateral should then be inserted, also well towards the back of the foam. These main lines indicate the final height and width of the design. Add decorative foliage as the design progresses, not forgetting some at the back so that, even though it is not visible, it does not look too stark – the design just might be placed in front of a mirror.

As you add more material, use it to echo and emphasise your first three lines. Keep the centre of balance well towards the back of the block, particularly for a display design. There may even be part of the block unused, but this is far better than bringing heavy stems too far forward which may result in the design falling flat on its face. This is no joke, it has happened!

Proportion will be dictated by the type of container and the situation of the arrangement. As a very rough guide, the main line should be not less than two-thirds the height of the container.

Width also depends on where the design is placed. The basic geometric shapes are helpful to keep in mind; the isosceles and the equilateral triangles. The first type can be designed with an exaggerated main line and shorter laterals: alternatively, with quite long laterals and a shorter central line. An example of this is a casket spray.

All-round designs

All-round designs are constructed on the five-point technique. This means that five stems of identical length are inserted into the base laterally and evenly-spaced, see figure 15. The length of these

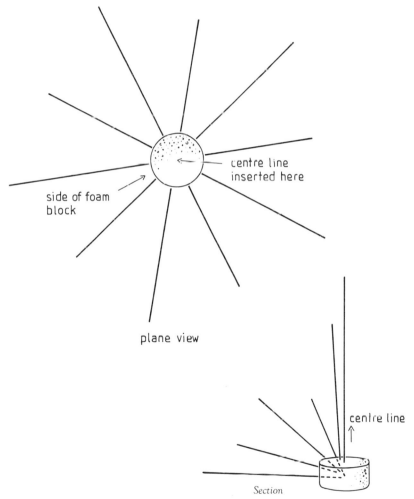

15 *All-round design*

five stems (they can be either flowers or foliage) determines the spread of area of the design. Place the vertical, this time right in the centre, which will indicate the final height of the arrangement. Insert another set of five stems, slightly above and between the first set. These will be shorter than the first five. Foliage should be added as the design progresses, but only enough to help mask and fill in, for the main lines must not be clouded. The single central flower may look, at this stage, somewhat stark. Add one or two more flowers of varying stem lengths to emphasise this central line.

Continue adding sets of five stems, each set shorter than the last, but do not crowd the design so that the flowers touch. The general effect should be specific in line with space between each flower.

The five-point foundation is used for smaller arrangements or when designing with larger flowers. A foundation of seven or even nine laterals may be used for much larger designs.

A charming variation on the open-style all-round design is the close posy-type made of mixed flowers. Unlike the traditional Victorian posy described in the wedding section, this centrepiece is built of almost any mixture of flowers, in fact the more colourful the better. It must still be planned with a basic bone formation which can be either five or seven laterals which will establish the area of the posy. A central flower is set to indicate the height, which should not be very tall, as the finished effect must be a gentle elipse. Other flowers and foliage are set in place, being inserted closely so that no stems are visible. This design makes an attractive table centrepiece. The main laterals should almost touch the surface on which the design is placed, the container will therefore not be visible, thus any shallow receptacle that holds water may be used.

The essence of this posy design is shape, form and colour. Mature and short-stemmed flowers can therefore be used to advantage. They last wonderfully well being set so closely. One idea for a 'Saturday Special'.

Asymmetrical arrangements

The word *symmetry* is defined as meaning in exact proportion, usually on either side of an actual or implied centre. *Asymmetrical* is the reverse, suggesting a lack of even-ness in each of the two parts. This is far more difficult to achieve than it sounds. For although the design is uneven, it still has an axis, a discernible point of origin. Figure 16.

Asymmetrical designs are appropriate for some display arrangements when using material with emphatically curved stems. The reverse also applies; that is, flowers with stiff straight stems will not work at all well in an asymmetrical design.

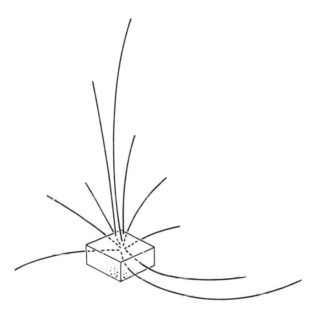

16 *Asymmetrical arrangement*

Method Decide on the position of the point of origin. Every stem should *seem* to emerge from here; obviously this is not possible, but the flow and the line must imply that they do. Is the lateral or the vertical to be the longer of the two main lines? Possibly the container itself may guide your decision, for obviously a design in a small container cannot have a very long lateral though, conversely, a design in a long-stemmed vase or on a candle holder will need a longer lateral to give the design visual balance.

After inserting the two main lines, that is, the first vertical and lateral, echo these with shorter inserts. Try not to crowd the centre with too much material, though, of course, the foam should be adequately masked.

Hospital arrangements

In general, try to choose a container that holds a fair amount of water. Always be sure to add a note to the card envelope reminding the recipient to add more water from time to time. Also make most designs slightly smaller and with material a little more closely packed than you would for a home or hotel arrangement. There is not often much space to spare in hospital and large flamboyant designs can sometimes be an embarrassment to the staff. The posy described earlier in this chapter is sometimes the most appropriate, for the mixture of flowers will provide interest; the design, as previously mentioned, lasts very well, while the flowers will fade at varying times and not all at once.

Whatever container is selected, make sure that it is completely stable. Overturned arrangements make extra work for the staff. If possible, choose flowers and foliage that do not drop and scatter. Unless specifically ordered, avoid dark flowers such as scarlet carnations, deep purple gladioli or red-brown chrysanthemums. And yes, it is a fact that a mixture of red and white flowers are not welcome in hospitals. This mixture may not worry the patients, but it causes definite concern amongst the staff.

Parallel form

Parallel form is a completely different concept from the radial facing and all-round designs previously described. Incidentally, asymmetrical arrangements also come under the heading of radial.

The technique of parallel form evokes natural growth, each stem having its own point of origin, as might be observed in a field of corn, a meadow of waving grass, or more formally, a flower bed. As mentioned in the section on wedding design, the trend is moving away from the formal, the contrived, towards a more natural look.

The container can be rectangular or circular. Soaked foam is cut to fit the area or pinholders can be used. In the simplest form of parallel design no stems are inserted laterally, therefore the foam need not project above the rim of the container.

Mask the foam with moss and/or small pebbles or some small foliage. Flowers are *set* (arranged is definitely not the appropriate word) in groups or they may even be inserted in a straight row, see figure 17. It must be emphasised that, commercially speaking, the

17 *Simple parallel design in a shallow circular container. Foam masked with moss*

traditional radial type of design is far more generally followed. But parallel form certainly has its place, being suited to such different environments as, for example, the front of a stage or platform, edging a pathway or church aisle or for a shallow window sill.

Decorative form
Material is arranged as the designer wishes, regardless of its natural growing season or habit. That is to say that the material is chosen for its colour and form, stems are cut to appropriate lengths to achieve the effect the designer has planned. The majority of traditional facing and all-round arrangements are constructed according to this form.

Vegetative form
This, in one way, is far more limiting to the designer, for all material must be selected according to its natural growing season and habit of growth. Thus, iris and daffodils could be arranged together, but the iris taller than the daffodils and all in parallel form, since, for these flowers, it is their habit to grow naturally straight. Roses and daffodils could not be put together, for their natural growing seasons vary. Vegetative design is very challenging as it forces the florist to consider the material not only in terms of colour, form and size, but also in terms of how and when it grows.

Using tubes and candles

Tubes of varying sizes are very useful for obtaining greater height in display designs. Usually made of plastic, they have a long spike that can be driven into the foam base. But for greater stability it is best to add one or two pieces of slender cane, thus making a firmer basis. Balanced on only one prong, the tube could begin to move and if this happens, the hole gets progressively larger and the tube more and more unstable.

To attach extra legs to the tube tape around the base of the tube. Tape a small portion of the split cane and then attach this portion to the base of the cone with yet more tape. Spread the three 'legs' and gently insert them into the foam. This gives far more reliable support to the cone than if all its weight is concentrated in one spot. It is not necessary to drive the legs right into the foam so that the base of the cone is resting on it. Greater height will be achieved if the cone is supported by these 'stilts' for, at whatever height, it is reliably stable. Obviously the larger the cone and the higher you want it, the stronger should be the supports. Do not forget to add water to the cone.

Candles are an elegant addition to many types of design. They are available in numerous different shapes, sizes and colours. Really large ones should be supported in the same manner as a cone, that is, on three lengths of split cane. The more slender ones can be supported with wire, perhaps taping two together for extra strength and stability. Small prongs about 5 cm long of wire 1.00 (19) or 1.25 (18) either single or double should be enough to support the very slender candles.

Candles should be carefully placed so that when they are lighted the flame does not damage the flowers. For Christmas window displays, the largest candles obtainable, supported with canes, look really impressive when used as the main verticals in a mixed arrangement.

Candle cups are a useful part of florist equipment, enabling you to make a design on a very slender base, such as a candle holder or a very narrow-necked vase. They are available in several sizes, usually finished in silver or gold or black. The base fits into the narrow aperture, rather like a cork into a bottle. If it is intended to be a permanent fixture it can be attached either with a glue gun or with a reliable fixative.

Also, *Oasis-fix* can be used to attach the candle cup to the base, but it is advisable to fix it well in advance of making the design. As has been mentioned elsewhere, the longer *Oasis-fix* is left, the stronger it will hold, though it never sets completely firmly. If it is necessary to remove a prong or anything else attached with this fixative, gently scrape most of it away with a knife. The residue can be cleaned off with white spirit.

NOTE   If the base is polished wood, silver or any material that might show damage, fix a strip of tape before attaching with *Oasis-fix*.

Glue gun   This is a very welcome addition to the florist's equipment. It has a multitude of uses and will often save valuable time. Be sure to buy one that does not drip and that, consequently, does not waste the glue sticks.

The foregoing probably seems to be a crushing amount of rules and regulations, for it is one thing to theorise on the basics of arrangement techniques; it is quite another matter to make them work. Most flowers and foliage rarely have uniformly straight stems: indeed our designs would be very dull if they did. So if you are a student-beginner, work at the outset with 'easier' materials such as carnations, spray chrysanthemums and iris. On the other hand, use any natural curve to your own advantage; never try to force a flower into a false position for it will certainly argue back by looking misplaced and uncomfortable.

Anniversaries

The florist frequently is asked for gift bouquets or arrangements for a silver wedding celebration. Apart from a golden wedding, few others are celebrated and it is useful if the florist knows some of these, maybe even advertising them to the clientele as a gentle reminder.

1st paper	9th willow	25th silver
2nd cotton	10th tin	30th pearl
3rd leather	11th steel	35th coral
4th flowers	12th silk	40th ruby
5th wood	13th lace	45th sapphire
6th candy	14th ivory	50th gold
7th wool	15th crystal	55th emerald
8th pottery	20th china	60th diamond
		70th platinum

Natural bunch or tied assembly   The objective is to make an arrangement that can be placed in a container without having to adjust or change the position of any of the material. In continental flower shops, all cut flowers are arranged like this as a matter of course, and learning to make these assemblies quickly plays an important part in student-training overseas.

The arrangement may be a completely round bunch, composed perhaps of only one or two kinds of flowers and foliage; it may be of mixed flowers or it could consist of one or two stems of very special blooms – anthuriums, for example – with exotic foliage and perhaps a curved branch for added textural interest and movement. Whatever the contents, the method of assembly is constant.

The material is assembled within one hand, piece by piece, the

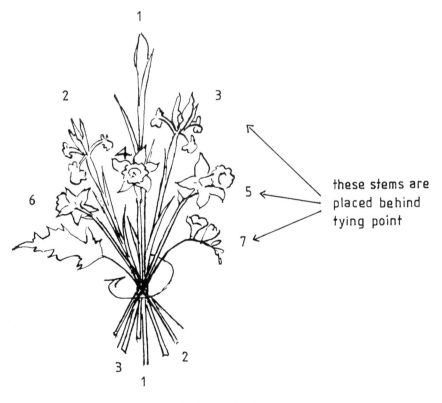

18 *Natural bunch*

finger-grip gradually relaxing as more stems are inserted. Foliage may be added from time to time to act as a cushion between some stems so that they do not swing out of place.

Having selected the material, clean all stems, placing both flowers and foliage into groups, according to their sorts. Add one stem at a time, always placing each flower in position and then guiding the stem to the 'holding' hand, so that every stem lays parallel with the others, thus eventually forming a spiral. Figure 18. Like most things done by an expert, assembling a natural bunch in the hand looks a simple matter. It is far from easy; long practice, muscular control and patience are demanded to perfect this apparently simple design. However, since none of the stems is anchored but just held within the hand, it is possible to change their position, to place and replace, though every stem must still lie parallel.

Finally, tie the bouquet very firmly at the holding point with about two twists of either raffia (baste) or binding string – never wire. Make sure that all the stems are quite clean and cut them all to the same length so that they can be stood in a vase of water.

6 Funeral tributes and sympathy designs

The impact of designs at a funeral can sometimes have unexpected and far-reaching results. People attending are usually in a very vulnerable state of mind. They are quick to appreciate an appealing tribute and are, understandably, equally quick to condemn a poor one.

It is absolutely vital that no effort is spared so that every single design, no matter how modest, looks fresh, crisp, as if it has just that moment been made.

Cards must be clearly written or typed, when not written by the client. They should be covered with a cellophane envelope or piece of film as protection from the weather. They should be fixed in a reasonably prominent position on the tribute so that people can easily read the inscription.

Types of bases and frames
Some florists still prefer to work exclusively with wire frames and moss. But ready-made frames are now available which not only help the florist by reducing the basic preparation work, but also help the flowers to last longer. There are several types on the market but the basic principle is much the same. The shape of the design is made of floral foam which is based either in a plastic frame or, as with a second type, is fixed to a polystyrene base. All these bases must, of course, be well soaked before beginning the design.

The polystyrene base is light brown; spray the edges, which are approximately 25.4 mm in depth with dark green *Oasis* spray paint. This will reduce the amount of masking needed. Wired edging foliage can be conveniently driven into the polystyrene thus leaving the total foam area for flowers and decorative foliage.

Mossing

Even if the majority of tributes are foam based, there are still some designs that have to be mossed, for example, a Vacant Chair (see page 71). This is a formal design which is still very popular in some areas; in fact, one can even have an upright chair or one with arms!

Moss should be damp before being wired to the frame. Wires will not drive easily into dry moss and to soak it after the frame has been prepared results, sometimes, in getting the wrong tension, for the base must be firm, yet not brick-hard; the student-florist learns how this should feel, for the tension has to be varied according to the size of tribute and the weight of material, flowers and foliage, to be used.

Tease the damp moss out into small piles, removing any foreign bodies such as small stones and sometimes little crawling things! With either bobbin wire or string, bind small handfuls to the frame as evenly as possible, see figure 19. Do not overmoss for this results in a heavy stodgy base. More moss can be added, if necessary, but it is not so easy to extract it once it has been firmly wired in place.

heap of moss teased out

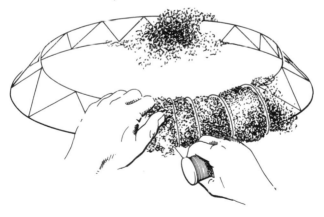

19 Mossing. *Apply small handfuls of moss and wire very firmly to frame, the binding being about 3 cm apart*

Informal tributes

These include the spray, the handsheaf, sympathy basket, a casket or coffin spray, and the posy wreath. These can all be constructed on the same lines as a flower arrangement. If foam bases are used, wiring is minimal.

Funeral spray This is composed of flowers and foliage arranged on a base. The principle is the same as for a facing design, except that the longest line is inserted laterally instead of vertically. The height at the visual point of origin should be not more than 30 cm for this measurement is approximately the clearance between the top of the casket (coffin) and the roof of a modern hearse. This applies to all tributes but to be quite certain in your area, check with the funeral directors locally.

The spray can also be based on a spray bar (wire) which has to be mossed and neatened at the back. All flowers and foliage must, consequently, be wired and mounted.

Handsheaf This design is constructed without a base. The finished shape is similar to the spray but all material is tied in the hand, with natural stems below the tying point. Flowers may be wired where necessary but the objective is to have a natural-looking design, yet with adequate control so that it can be handled with comfort. See figures 20 and 21. Select strong support foliage and also, so far as possible, flowers with strong stems that will not need wire.

Bind very tightly with string, attaching each flower and piece of foliage separately so that everything stays in place. The back of the sheaf should be quite flat. Flowers towards the tying point may have to be wired in order to give some elevation. Insert some foliage with several flowers as a returned end (see figure 34), so that the tying point does not look too stark. Finally, attach a ribbon bow. In width and colour this should be in keeping with the flowers; not so wide that it overpowers the design nor so narrow that it looks like an afterthought. Make sure that all stems are clean, free from foliage, wires or thorns.

Sympathy basket The traditional shape is rectangular. They come in several sizes and have good firm handles and a solid base. Some have their own inner plastic liners; others do not, and these must be fitted with a liner before beginning work. There are other designs of basket available which can also be used when appropriate; for example, if several baskets are to go to one funeral, it is unprofessional to send them all looking the same.

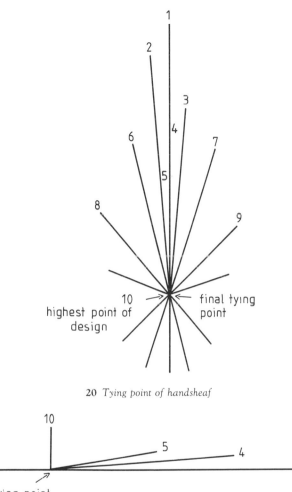

1

2

3

4

6

7

5

8

9

10 →← final tying
point
highest point of
design

20 *Tying point of handsheaf*

10

5

4

1

tying point

21 *Section*

22 *Sympathy basket*

As with any flower arrangement the size of foam block will be governed by the size and weight of flower stems. When using the rectangular basket, the block should stand only about 2.5 cm proud of the rim – no higher or the central material will be too near the handle, thus leaving no space for the hand to grasp it.

If designing with heavy-headed flowers, such as gladioli or chrysanthemums, add wire mesh over the foam for greater support. Secure the mesh to the handle either with tape or a piece of wire, see figure 23.

23 *Attaching handle to sympathy basket*

If possible, pack damp moss around the foam, partly for appearance and also to help stabilise it. Having masked the foam, insert the first two long laterals as low down in the block as possible. These stems should be completely horizontal which means that there is very little depth of foam to work with, but, as previously mentioned, the higher the foam is above the rim of the basket, the nearer the flower heads will be to the handle. It is essential that space is left for the hand to grasp the design by the handle. Although the two ends of the design need not be a precise mirror image one of another, they must have actual balance so that when the basket is lifted it does not tip.

A ribbon bow can be added to the base of the handle; never higher. The mourning card should also be attached to this point. All cards attached to funeral tributes should be supported across the back with wire, to prevent the card curling in a damp atmosphere. See figure 24.

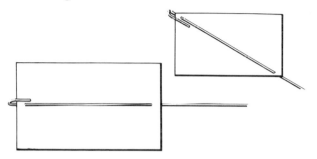

24 *Attaching cards*

Work method for sympathy basket
1 Prepare ribbon, wire card and write destination label
2 Select basket
3 Prepare inner lining with *Oasis-fix*, a prong and well-soaked foam
4 Attach wire mesh if neeeded and fix firmly to handles
5 Mask foam
6 Select flowers and foliage

Double-ended spray   The two ends of this design need not necessarily be identical, although they usually are the same length. There are several bases specifically designed for this type of tribute. The spray can also be made on a foam block fixed very securely to a plastic tray. First attach some narrow strips of draught excluder across the underside of the tray. This will prevent the tribute from sliding when the coffin is moved.

The foam block should be attached on two prongs, and also taped around for extra security. This type of tribute is generally fairly lavish so it is prudent to make absolutely sure that the base is very firm before beginning the arrangement. Mask the base and begin the design by establishing the full length and then the height (not more than 20 cm).

Posy wreath   The base for this design is called a *posy pad*. It can also be made, like an all-round arrangement, on foam secured to a plastic saucer or other suitable container. And provided the material is wired and mounted, it can be designed on a moss base.

Work method for a posy wreath
1 Prepare ribbon (not obligatory); wire card and write destination label
2 If using polystyrene base, spray edge dark green
3 Insert wired foliage to edge and mask top foam
4 Establish width of design by placing first five stems
5 Mark the centre
6 Add more groups of flowers and foliage, recessing some so that the design does not look too formal. The outline should be a shallow curve; thus, the centre flower should not be placed too high

Sheaves in cellophane   Cut flowers packed in paper and cellophane bags are sometimes ordered for funerals. In some areas this is still a usual type of informal tribute. The thought is that the flowers shall afterwards be taken to a hospital or old people's home.

There are several reasons, both ethical and artistic, why this sort of tribute is not particularly successful. The cellophane-fronted paper bags not only mist over when the flowers are tied within, but the paper backing gradually disintegrates. Moreover, a cellophane presentation is more generally associated with giftwrap and, as such, could be thought to be out of context at a funeral.

Some funeral directors tolerate this variety of tribute; others dislike it intensely and some even remove the bags before the ceremony. They find that sometimes the flowers are not tied *within* the covering and when this is removed, the flowers just fall apart. Therefore if this type of informal tribute has to be prepared, it should be done as follows:

Method   Prepare a ribbon bow with long tying ends. Select suitable foliage and cut it to a suitable length. Remove all heavy woody stems. Style the flowers and foliage into an attractive bunch and tie with the ribbon.

Very gently insert the bunch into the bag, leaving the bow outside. Gather the sides of the bag inwards at the tying point and tie securely either behind the bow or in between the loops.

7 Funeral tributes: formal designs

Edging
Not every formal design requires an edging, though its main purpose is both to protect the flowers and to provide a finish to the design. This can be prepared with ribbon, net or any suitable water-resistant fabric. There are a number of foliages suitable for edging and any is valid provided it has good lasting quality. Cupressus, laurel and camellia are all excellent for the purpose. Cupressus is probably the most widely used.

Method Cut cupressus carefully so that small pieces can be formed into 'fans'. The size depends on the dimension of the tribute but a good average is about 6 cm finished length. Long pieces of edging will not look neat and crisp and will detract from the formal appearance of the design. This is repetitive work; it is also time-consuming, but cupressus edging can be prepared at any time when there is a break in shop activities. It will last for several weeks if the fans are laid in rows, one on top of the other in any small box; for example, one about the size of a violet or anemone box. It does not require to be oversprayed but the box should be kept in a cool place.

Gather several pieces into one hand and secure them with wire .90 or .70 (20 and 22) length not less than 12.5 cm, using the *loop method*. Make the loop with one end longer than the other. Lay loop against the base of the little flat bunch of cupressus. Holding both loop and foliage in one hand, bind the longer end of wire twice around both loop and foliage. Note that the two binds are separate, that is, not one on top of the other, see figure 25.

Laurel edging Clean and grade foliage so that similar-sized leaves are grouped together. Take three and fold them with the upper surface of the leaf inside. Hold them gently by the base and do not make a crease or crack along the centre of the leaves. Drive

25 *Wiring – loop method*

a wire .90 or .70 (20 or 22) through the base of these three leaves so that they are secured at the base and form a fan at the tips. Wind one end of the wire around the other as well as around the base and/or small stems of the leaves.

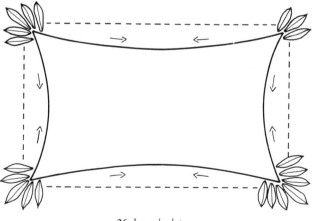

26 *Laurel edging*

Ribbon edging   Make pleats and secure each one with a stapler. Knife pleats are made by folding one piece of ribbon and securing it with a staple, and, working *away* from the first pleat, making another fold the same size as the first one. Continue until the length is sufficient. As a guide to measurements, at least three times the overall edge-length is necessary for either knife or box pleats. See figure 27.

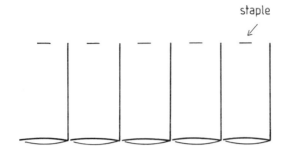

27 *Ribbon edging (knife pleats)*

Box pleating   The ribbon is first folded as if for a knife pleat; a similar fold is made so that the two folds meet: that is, one pleat facing left and one facing right, see figure 28. Continue this process, but do not leave any gaps between the folds. This is a most attractive edging: it has more dimension than knife pleating, which is flatter. Whenever possible, work directly from the bolt of ribbon so as to be sure (a) that you have sufficient length and (b) so that none is wasted.

Ribbon is attached to the base in several ways: with a reliable glue gun, with large steel pins or with double hairpins (known as *German pins*), or by means of a large staple gun. If using pins, drive them in on the diagonal so that they do not easily pull out.

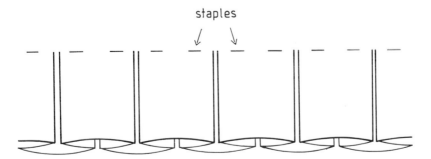

28 *Box pleating*

Backing

All mossed bases should be neatened at the back or underside. The quickest way to neaten a wreath or cross is to bind pieces of cupressus on, taking care to cut away most of the woody stem. Bind to the back of the cross, beginning at each of the four ends and working towards the centre, in the same way as the moss is applied.

A cushion, pillow, heart or any other solid design is backed with foliage which must be pinned on. Laurel is very suitable, though any strong long-lasting foliage in season may be used. Collect similar-sized leaves, taking about four at a time and with their tips exactly together, pile them one on top of the other. The leaves can be different lengths, but they should be as uniform in width as possible. Holding the tips firmly together between finger and thumb, cut the base of the leaves neatly away. They should then all be the same length, see figure 29(a).

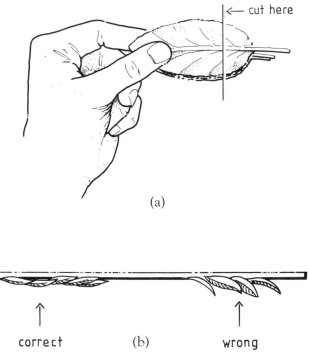

29 *Cutting leaves for backing*

Pins Cut wires .70 (22) or .90 (20) into short lengths to form hairpins. Beginning at the edge of the design, pin the leaves, one pin to every leaf, working towards the spot where the top spray will eventually be positioned. Pin the leaves closely for they must not bend backwards as the tribute is lifted up. Figure 29(b). Cupressus or other foliage can also be pinned on in the same way.

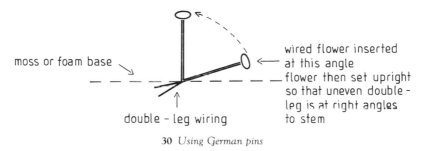

30 *Using German pins*

Fixing the foam block for a top spray The foam block for a finishing spray must be attached before any base flowers are inserted.

For mossed bases, attach as follows: bend two wires exactly in half, 1.00 or 1.25 (19 or 18), length 34 cm. Turn the base upsidedown and drive the wires through to approximately the spot where the top spray will be. Each double wire should be inserted about 2 cm apart.

Turn the base over and drive both wires right through as far as they will go. Impale the soaked foam block on to the wires and gently ease the block down so that it rests firmly on the design base.

Place two small pieces of stick or stem between each pair of wires to prevent the wire from biting into the foam. Holding the stem firmly, twist the two wires round one another over the stem so that the foam block is firm on the base. This is quite difficult to do single-handed. If someone can steady the stem then two hands can be applied to the wires and a much firmer twist results. If the block is not completely firm, the only solution is to begin again for it is useless to design on an unstable base. See figures 31 and 32.

Fixing top spray foam block to foam base
Method (1) With a glue gun *before* either base or foam block is soaked. Alternatively attach it as described for mossed bases.
Method (2) Cover spray block with nylon netting. Pin the netting down very firmly to the design base using German pins.

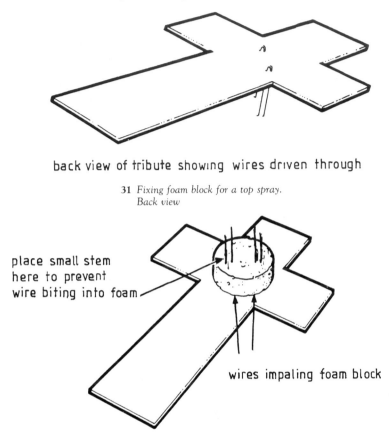

back view of tribute showing wires driven through

31 *Fixing foam block for a top spray.*
Back view

place small stem
here to prevent
wire biting into foam

wires impaling foam block

32 *Fixing foam block for a top spray*

Formal designs on mossed bases

Cross Begin mossing at each of the four ends, working towards the centre. The ends should be very firm and as square as possible. A wire cross frame longer then 1 m may tend to 'whip' with the weight of moss and flowers. It is advisable to attach a strong cane right down the centre before binding on the moss. Moss over the cane so that the back of the frame is still flat, see figure 33.

Neaten the back of the frame, working from the ends of the arms towards the centre, but leave the centre open until the foam block for the top spray has been attached. Then finish this section off so that the wires are hidden.

Edge the frame, taking care not to drive any wires through to

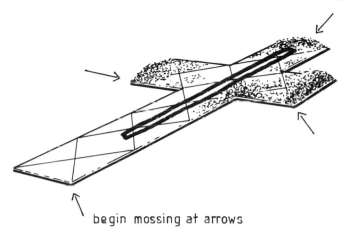

begin mossing at arrows

33 *Formal design on mossed base*

the back of the frame, thus spoiling your neat backing. Drive each wire *across* the frame and return the end firmly into the moss, see figure 34.

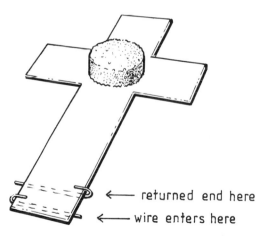

←— returned end here

←— wire enters here

34 *Edging the frame*

Solid-based cross   Insert prepared flowers, beginning at the centre and working towards the ends of each arm. The size of the flowers as well as the dimensions of the tribute will determine how many flowers there should be in each row. Ideally, the flowers will all be the same size, but this is hardly likely. If there is a noticeable variation, group them in sizes and save the smaller ones for the edges. You will have more control over the shape using smaller flowers, for the clear lines of the design must be maintained regardless of what flowers are being used.

One other vital point – do make absolutely sure that you have enough flowers for the base. This may seem really too elementary a point to make here, but solid-based designs consume a great deal of material. It is possible to place a row or two of flowers as a trial run, without fixing them. Then do some multiplication and it should be possible to estimate the final number to within a few blooms. The same comment, of course, applies to other solid-based designs: cushion, pillow and heart. If you are obliged to introduce another type of flower or colour, do it so that it seems that it was planned all the time, that is, try to make a logical pattern.

Flowers for the inside rows can be pinned in on a double-leg mount (see wiring). Insert each flower as shown on figure 30. The edge flowers should have an uneven leg mount so that one end of wire just bites into the moss and the longer one can be driven into the moss at an angle, emerging out on the opposite side of the design, see figure 34 for edging.

Top spray Mask the foam block as if for a flower arrangement. The spray should be significant but must not cover more than one-third the total area of the base. This applies to all solid bases. The spray may be designed on the diagonal or to echo the formal lines of the cross, see figure 35.

Open cross on mossed base Design should be edged, neatened at the back and the top side lightly masked. Flowers and foliage are inserted so that there is space between each. But the clear shape of the design must still be seen.

Method Select main flowers and, beginning in the centre, set these in at suitable intervals. Large flowers, such as iris or carnations should have at least the space of one flower between each one. Check the levels of the blooms for they should all be level. Figure 36. Their height will be governed by the size of the tribute. The final outline should be gently bevelled, see figure 37.

Next put in the outline flowers, adding small pieces of decorative foliage to help furnish the area. Thirdly set in the 'bridging level' between the main and the outline flowers. If these three levels do not describe a gentle curve probably the main flowers are too high.

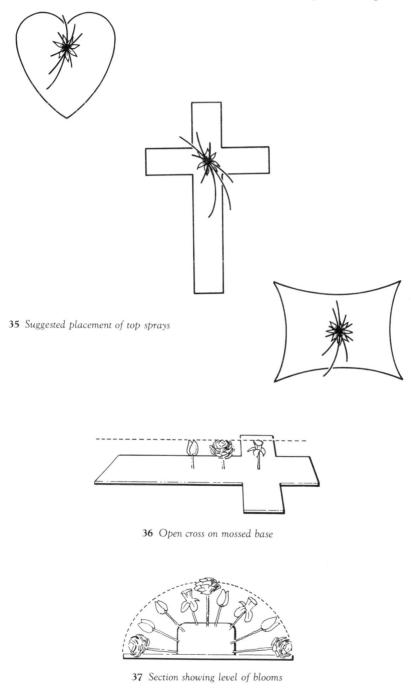

35 Suggested placement of top sprays

36 Open cross on mossed base

37 Section showing level of blooms

Avoid crowding the design, but, on the other hand, there should be sufficient material for the finished effect to be valid. While flowers at level 1 (the edge flowers) should be all the same, also those at level 3 (the main flowers); the rest can be varied in shape, size, texture and colour.

Foam-based cross   It is not necessary to neaten the reverse, but you may like to apply dark green *Oasis* spray to the polystyrene bases.

With the exception of the edge flowers and foliage, which should be wired to be quite certain they stay in position, only wire other materials that will not drive easily into the foam. Insert all stems, whether wired or not, as firmly as possible; they must not fall out when the design is handled.

Wreath, solid base on moss   Follow the same preparation guidelines as for the cross.

NOTE   Not all solid-based tributes need have a top spray. In fact, some look more dignified as a beautiful evenly-set ring – the traditional symbol of eternity.

Open based designs

The open wreath, moss or foam base   Select the main flowers and insert them at even intervals round the frame, exactly vertical. Begin with either five, seven or nine, according to (a) the size of the flower, and (b) the dimension of the wreath. Next define the outer edge with double the number of main flowers. These should be set at even intervals around the outer ring. The length of these stems will determine the final diameter of the wreath. Thus a design with final diameter of 45 cm can be made on a frame measuring only 25 cm.

Set an inner circle of flowers on very short stems so that the shape of the ring is still apparent. Place these between the main flowers and almost at right angles to them. Recess other flowers and fill in with decorative foliage where necessary, taking care not to overcrowd the design, for its form should be completely distinctive from the solid-based wreath or cross. The open wreath and cross are very popular designs for, with a limited number of 'master' flowers and sufficient support material, the florist can make the tribute look not only very attractive, but also expensive and lavish in appearance.

Gates of Heaven. How to moss. Cut a piece of heavy cardboard or polystyrene exactly to fit the base. Next turn the frame upside down and fill the base with moss, pressing it down firmly. Then cover the moss with foil or other waterproof material and fit the supporting base over. This, obviously, is to restrain the moss when the frame is turned right side up again. Make several small holes in the cardboard and attach it firmly to the wire frame with short stub wires, 1.25 (18) or 1.00 (19). Turn the frame right side upward and check that the base is really firm. Figure 38.

Bind moss to the arch very finely and evenly, remembering that when flowers are added it should not seem to be too wide and stodgy. Paint the gates and the cross gold. A small top spray can be added to one side. A white dove completes the design.

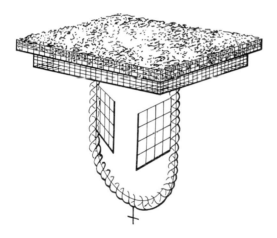

38 *Gates of Heaven (inverted)*

Vacant Chair   Moss the seat in the same way as the base for the Gates of Heaven. The chair back and legs should be mossed very finely so that they still appear in proportion even with flowers added. Obviously very small flowers must be used, which is time-consuming. It is usual to add a flower spray; this should be quite small otherwise the shape and detail of the chair will be obscured.

How to moss cushion and pillow   These bases are in two sections; a flat base and the top, which is curved. Cut some neat pieces of cupressus or other suitable foliage and lay it generously on the base. This foliage will not only prevent the moss from coming through the rather wide mesh but will also give a neat finish. Thus when money and time is at a premium, it may not be necessary to back the design as well. Next bind some moss to the corners of the cushion and pillow base. Figure 39. This is to ensure that they are firm enough to support the edging foliage and flowers. However, the moss should not be so thick that the top section will not join closely to it.

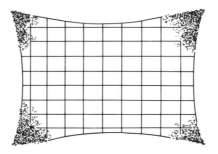

39 *Binding the corners with moss*

Fill in the rest of the frame with moss. A beginner-florist may possibly put in far too much at first. It is, in fact, easier to add more, even when the two sections have been wired together, rather than having to extract it.

Place the two sections together and fix firmly with wire at the corners and once or twice along each side. Twist the wires together with pliers so as to get a close join at the two edges. The centre of the design should feel springy to the touch, while the corners, though thinner, should feel more solid.

Fix the foam base in position for the spray. Set flowers at each corner first, working towards the centre of the curved edge and still maintaining the shape. When the edges are complete, check that each corner is in line by placing the design on the floor and looking down on it directly from above. Fill in the rest of the base, working towards the top spray area.

Method The logical work method for preparing cushion and pillow designs on a wire frame is as follows:
1 Line base with foliage
2 Wire moss to corners
3 Fill remainder of base with moss
4 Fix top firmly to base

5 Check amount of moss in centre of design. Enough or too much?
6 Fix foam block for top spray
7 Edge design with ribbon or foliage
8 Insert flowers at each corner
9 Complete edges, then check that corners are level and also that edges are still nicely curved
10 Complete flower base, working towards top spray area
11 Design spray
12 Attach memorial card

The work method for making cushion and pillow designs on foam bases begins at point 6. However, since these bases are flat, it will be necessary for the florist to make the gentle curve towards the centre by using longer-stem flowers.

Heart on moss base   This also is constructed like a moss sandwich. First line the flat base with foliage and bind some moss to the point of the shape. Then follow directions 3 to 11. Figure 40.

40 *Heart on moss base*

Heart on foam base   Follow work-programme beginning at item 6. Insert flowers at point first, then from the top around the two lobes and joining up at approximately points X. Figure 41.

41 *Heart on foam base*

How to moss an Open Book The frame is constructed with a flat base and a curved top, which are already joined, leaving a gap in between. This must be filled with moss as evenly as possible which is not easy since it has to be pushed in small quantities through the holes in the mesh.

Fix the foam block for the top spray and then neaten the back of the design.

Small white or gold flowers are neatly pinned to the sides to resemble the gilt edges of the pages. If small flowers are not available, foliage could be substituted.

The top of the design (the open pages) is usually based in white, but there should be a clear definition between the open page and the edge.

Design the top spray and add a ribbon to simulate the book mark. The spray should be small so as not to detract from the overall shape of the design. When quoting a price for an Open Book, bear in mind that in terms of material it is really the equivalent of two cushions. Figure 42.

Suggested flowers for solid bases
Spray chrysanthemums; hydrangea; violet; daffodil; dahlia; narcissus; hyacinth; asters; anemones; ranunculus; stock; scabious; sweet sultan. Any suitable foliage may be used for a set base.

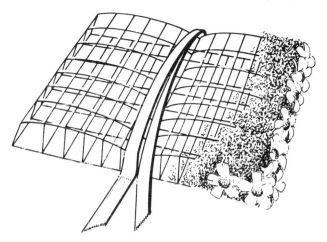

42 *Mossing an Open Book*

Foliage also makes a very attractive base; the top spray of special flowers looking all the more significant against the green background.

Laurel pinning
This is a technique that demands precision and practice as well as a good deal of patience. Laurel is a long-lasting foliage that is particularly useful for memorial designs. Select only mature leaves for the young ones will quickly go limp! Figures 43 and 44.

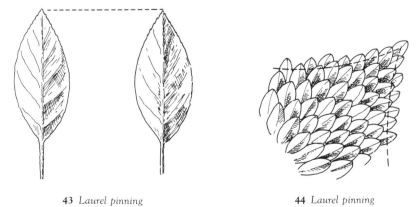

leaf tips must be perfect

43 *Laurel pinning*   **44** *Laurel pinning*

Choose those that are perfect at the tip, discarding any that are mis-shapen or damaged. Group them for uniformity as described in the section on edging. Cut wire hairpins .70 (22) about 3 cm long when doubled over.

Group and cut the leaves as described in the section on laurel edging. Pin every leaf separately, making sure that it is in the correct position before fixing it. Whatever the design, make sure the outline is precise. When working on a curve, save the larger leaves for the outer edge and the smaller ones for the inside. Overlap every leaf generously so that only the top 2 cm are visible. Make sure, also, that no pin can be seen.

From time to time, check the outline by turning the base over to see if the length of leaf is constant both on the outer and inner curves of the design. If a top spray is planned, fix the foam block and then work towards this area.

When all leaves are secured, wipe the design with a damp *Kleenex* tissue and apply a light spray of *Leafshine* or similar preparation.

Chaplet   This is popular in some areas as a memorial design. It is also suitable as a funeral tribute, particularly when a formal design

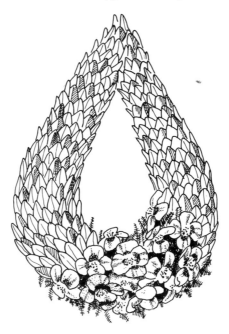

45 *Chaplet*

is wanted, and as something different from the traditional cross or wreath. It is available as a foam base as well as in several sizes in wire. These, of course, must be prepared with moss. Figure 45. The design can be followed as a solid base of flowers of all one kind, with or without edging and a top spray. Another alternative is a base of foliage (laurel is particularly suitable) with a top spray of flowers or special foliage.

Sometimes it is made as an open design with mixed flowers, on the same method as for an open cross or wreath. But most people find the formal base more appealing.

A memorial chaplet is frequently based with laurel and finished with a ribbon in the appropriate ceremonial colours. It is also used as a remembrance tribute at Christmas with a laurel base and top spray of mixed holly and foliage and berry.

In essence, a very versatile and adaptable design, which should always be in the florist's repertoire.

8 Buttonholes, corsages and head-dresses

Buttonholes

What do people expect when they order a buttonhole or lapel spray? Whatever the choice of flowers, one point is certain. The flowers should last well and stand up to being worn or handled, probably in a warm atmosphere. This adds up to three things: that the flowers should be top quality, that they are well-conditioned and that they are properly wired and assembled.

Another reply to our original rhetorical question is that people expect, in fact, what they order. For it does not always follow that the person that books the order makes the design. Therefore the florist should thoroughly understand what is wanted before beginning work. This sounds extremely elementary and in any case, how can anyone possibly make a mistake with a buttonhole? A single flower, for sure, and probably itemised whether carnation, rose or other suitable flower. But what type of foliage, or none at all, maybe? For a lady or gentleman? For a wedding or for a dinner party? if so, is it 'white tie and tails' or dinner jacket (smoking), for generally it is a white flower if the first but a coloured one for the second?

A further prerequisite of flowers that are worn – and this applies to a single flower for a gentleman's lapel just as forcefully as it applies to the most elaborate shoulder spray – is that the design shall be as light as possible; an adjunct to the outfit that enhances it rather than being worn as a penance.

Gentleman's buttonhole A carnation is still top favourite and most people prefer no foliage. Some still insist on a little asparagus fern; this must be wired loop method and then taped in with the wired flower stem. A buttonhole worn by a man should have one stem only, not much more than 7 to 8 cm long. Finish with dark green tape and add one straight pin, so that it can be fixed immediately on receipt.

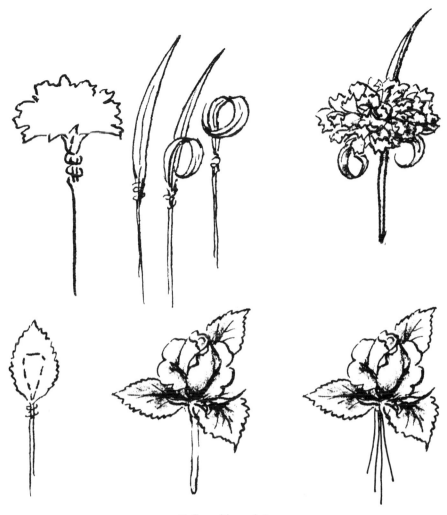

46 *Formal buttonholes*

A rose buttonhole for a man sometimes has a few leaves added around the flower, either ivy or small rose leaves. Wire rose leaves in pairs, that is, two together which creates a more solid lasting fabric than if they are wired singly. Obviously the two leaves must be similar in size.

Buttonhole for a lady This may contain exactly the same material as for a man but the finish is a little different. Each piece of foliage is wired and taped separately. The design is then assembled in the hand and bound tightly together at the holding point, just under the flower. Two firm twists of fine silver wire will hold it safely together. Overbind this wire with tape and the lapel spray is complete. Figure 46 illustrates the difference in finish. The same applies whatever flower is chosen. Any relatively flat bloom is suitable for a buttonhole; a tiny dahlia, double or single spray chrysanthemum, a small orchid: so long as the material will last reliably, let your imagination inspire you away from the traditional carnation.

Corsages

Corsages may be composed of one or two flowers with some suitable foliage, or they can be assembled as a truly high-style design of elaborately-blended buds, florets, foliage and may be berries. This is one area in which the designer's creative ability can sometimes be allowed full rein. It could be regarded as an item of living jewelry: therefore it must be just right, neither too modest for the occasion nor overdone, so that the wearer is embarrassed. The question of a ribbon trimming occurs, and this is frequently a decision that is dictated by area preference. Some clients believe the design is not complete without a small bow; yet others detest a bow and prefer even an opulent cattleya orchid corsage finished simply with foliage. The florist tries to please all of the people all of the time, and it does help in this objective to execute the order as accurately as possible.

Assemble a corsage or shoulder spray on similar lines to making a bouquet, for, in effect, it is indeed a miniature bouquet. Decide on the overall size of the design and build some of the material into units, taping them right to the ends of the mount wires. At this stage it could be emphasised that, unlike the bouquet, it is not always essential to build the unit on to a support wire. As an example, if three or four pieces of material are wired on .46 (26) and are then taped together to form the unit, the combined weight build-up of several 46 (26) wires may be sufficient support without adding another heavier wire.

However, all the same principles of design should be applied. Actual balance, in particular, is all-important. For the spray will, possibly, be attached to a delicate dress fabric; it must not damage nor drag the neckline out of shape, neither should it feel too heavy. In fact, once pinned into position, the perfect spray should be completely forgotten by the wearer.

Prayerbook spray

This is a corsage-type design that must be assembled in relation to the size of the book. That is to say, while the design should be significant, it must not totally overpower the prayerbook. The design will most likely be long and slender, with a returned end (see figure 34). The point of origin should be in the exact place where the bride will hold the book, which is usually towards the lower edge rather than in the centre.

Probably the bride will have brought the book to the shop several days or weeks previous to the wedding date. Wrap it carefully, label it with name and date of wedding and give her a receipt, for it is usually a relatively expensive article and may also have some sentimental value to her.

Place a long strip of white satin ribbon as a book marker in the marriage service section, also another length across the first page. Never use polypropylene ribbon for this occasion.

Try to trim away as much excess wire as possible during assembly of the design, so that the binding point is as delicate as it possibly can be. When all is complete extend the handle by adding more wires so that eventually the handle measures about the same length as the book cover, plus another 2 cm. Finish this extended handle with tape, either pale green or white.

Bend the handle very sharply from the binding point so that it is parallel with the design. Slide the book cover carefully between the flowers and the handle. Bend the tip of the handle back over the top edge of the cover so that it grips the top unit of the design, and re-arrange flowers and foliage so that this small piece of taped wire is not visible. Figure 47.

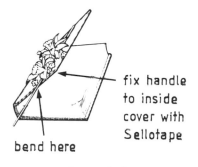

fix handle
to inside
cover with
Sellotape

bend here

47 *A prayer book spray*

The spray should then be quite firm and it ought to be possible for the bride to open the book without the flowers moving. If a little more security seems to be needed, fix the handle to the inside of the cover with a small strip of *Sellotape*.

The 'Cathedral' prayerbook slide which can be obtained from the accessory wholesalers can be attached to the cover of the prayerbook. The spray is then clipped to the slide.

A unit

A unit, whether simple or multiple, is the basis for the majority of designs such as bouquets, handsprays, decorations for a fan or parasol, a handbag or hat ornamentation, also for large shoulder sprays. Never overload one unit with too many flowers or leaves, for this may result in both visual and actual weight being in the wrong place. It could also 'decentralise' control over the placement of some material.

Tape only flowers to one unit, leaves to another. Thus each should be built into separate units which can, however, then be joined together.

Circlet head-dresses

One of the few exceptions to the above concept is the circlet head-dress which is assembled either in two units or on one continuous unit.

Method 1 Tape the end 2 cm of a .56 (24) wire. Bend it into a loop and tape the end in securely to the wire. Divide prepared material for the circlet into two equal parts and working from one section of material only, place the first bud, flower or leaf so that it overlaps the loop. Continue taping material in closely, to this one unit adding another .56 (24) wire when necessary. Cut off spare wire from prepared materials to prevent the design from becoming too heavy, both in weight and finish. Curve the unit as it proceeds, possibly taping in a little more material to the outer curve.

Work as far as the centre and if you would like this to be a little more significant, add more material binding it in tightly with silver wire, so as not to get a build-up of tape on one spot.

Prepare a second .56 (24) wire but leave about 2 cm taped ready to form a hook. Place the first piece of material almost to the end of the wire so that when the hook is made the two end flowers or leaves will just meet. Tape material from the second group into the unit as nearly as possible in the same sequence as the first one. Curve this unit the reverse way from the first one, adding material until both sides are the same length. Cut the wire 'handles' down to about 2.5 cm and tape neatly. Then push the two centres together very tightly so that the little taped handles cross. Bind together with silver wire once or twice very tightly at this point.

Finally tape each handle to the back of the unit. It will be necessary to separate the flowers to do this. A little time and patience are needed for this final join, but it is worth while to get a neat finish.

To fix Curve the circlet around so that the two ends are touching. Hook the straight end of wire through the loop and secure. If wanted, fix ribbon streamers to these two points.

Method 2 Having measured the required length of the head-dress, prepare a .56 (24) wire base, taping the first end into a loop as in method 1. It will be necessary to join wires to get the length. Overlap them slightly but keep the finish as slender and light as possible.

Mark the centre of the wire and divide material into two equal sections. Tape material in as before, working from one end towards the centre and then from the other end. Have a little extra material handy to add to the centre if needed.

Finish as for method 1.

Everlasting flowers and foliage
Silk and polyester (fabric) flowers and foliage and dried material
The same techniques can be applied when working with everlasting as with fresh material. Small florets, leaves, buds, etc, can be wired and taped, ready for assembly into units. The stems of some dried material are very brittle. Tape first, then wire and tape again, then the binding wire will not cut the stem. The stems of some fabric flowers are not very elegant so the flowers must be removed and, in most instances, wired as if for a fresh flower and then taped.

Arrangements Not only are the stems of some fabric flowers unconvincing in appearance, but some are too whippy to support the flower head. They should be supported with extra wire or split cane and then taped over. Remember always to use the proper dry foam when designing with dried or fabric flowers and foliage. The type that has to be soaked for fresh flowers is not so solid in texture and may break up with the weight of the material. The dry foam can also be masked with green moss which will dry out in time and still retain its fresh green colour.

For a dried arrangement, mask the foam with grey moss, sometimes known as *Icelandic* or *reindeer moss*. This has to be soaked in clean water when it will fluff up like a sponge. Once pinned on the foam block it will gradually dry out and seem to be part of the design. Try to blend the masking material to the flowers. If they are primarily cream to amber to dark brown, use the reindeer moss. On the other hand, if they are fresh flowers dried to natural colour – for example, roses and delphiniums – the green moss is more appropriate.

Mixing fresh and everlasting material   In bouquets and other designs made up in the hand, there is no problem, for each piece or unit of material is built into the design where needed. In arrangements, if possible, the two should be kept separate. Thus, if the majority of the design is composed of everlasting material, any fresh flowers and foliage should be in a cone with water.

9 Weddings

A bouquet, handspray or a posy are really stylised variations of the natural bunch. For example, when someone picks a few flowers, the stems are usually all held within one hand and the flowers face more or less where they will. But wherever the flower head may be, the stem passes through the hand; that is, if the flower is still part of the bunch.

A bouquet should be assembled so that the stem of every piece of material *appears* to spring from, or join to, the binding point, that is, the point of origin or heart of the design. It is, of course, an optical illusion: rather, it is a question of angle and flow of the material, see figure 48 which shows the right and wrong way of building a unit of ivy leaves. Thus, if the leaf or flower does not appear to be invisibly attached to the heart of the design, that particular piece of material seems to be disembodied or detached from the point of origin (the binding area).

Bouquet bases
These are very popular with some florists as the flowers and foliage can be inserted into a soaked foam base, as if for a flower arrangement. It is, however, a very special technique which should never be attempted without having first completely understood the assembly techniques of making the bouquet in the hand.

Bouquet handles
Method 1   Approximately 1 m of ribbon is required to finish a bouquet handle, plus a bow with two tying ends, each about 30 cm long.

Attach one end of the ribbon to the handle, exactly at the binding point with *Sellotape*. Bind to the base of the handle, pulling tightly at an angle of 45 degrees, which should cause the ribbon to stretch slightly (on the cross). Bind to a fraction beyond the tip of the handle, turn the ribbon and bind back upwards towards the design, still stretching the ribbon as much as possible. Secure with *Sellotape*. Tie the ribbon bow over this point.

Method 2　Cut a length of ribbon about 1 m long. Prepare a small matching bow, securing it with a taped wire .56 (24). Position the bow exactly at the binding point at the back of the design. Tape it in position firmly and continue taping to the end of the handle.

48 *Building a unit of ivy leaves*

Place one end of the binding ribbon *behind* the bow, leaving an end about 30 cm long. Press the bow firmly back against the binding area, thus securing the ribbon.

Bind the longer strip of ribbon down and then up the handle as in method 1. When the bow is reached, bend it forwards so that the ribbon end can be passed behind it. The two tying ends will then be crossed behind the bow, one to the left (the first one) and the other to the right of the bow.

Press the bow firmly back into position; turn the bouquet around and tie the two ends in a single knot and then a neat bow. See figures 49, 50 and 51.

Suggested method for bridal work
1 Prepare packing material and put a bouquet stand ready in case one is obliged to leave the design
2 Prepare ribbons
3 Wire and tape foliage and build into units
4 Wire and tape flowers and assemble into units, so far as possible
5 Assemble design. NOTE: if several versions of one design are being made, eg three bridesmaids' handsprays or three head-dresses, wire and tape all material, store it in separate polythene bags and then assemble all at once
6 Spray designs (mist) and pack immediately

Suggested work programme
For a wedding consisting of fifteen buttonholes for gentlemen, five special corsages, head-dresses for three bridesmaids, their bouquets, a cake top and the bridal bouquet the following programme is suggested:

1 Complete all buttonholes and corsages
2 Prepare flowers and foliage for bridesmaids' head-dresses and also their bouquets
3 Make the head-dresses, then the bouquets
4 Make the cake top (this sometimes has to be delivered either on the wedding-eve or early in the morning for placement on the cake
5 Make the bridal bouquet last of all so that it looks 'morning-fresh'

Wiring and taping techniques have been discussed in the chapter dealing with this subject. Here we will describe methods of assembly only.

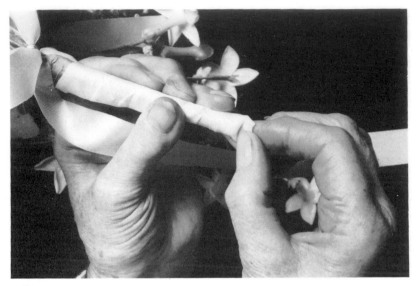

49

50

49–51 *Finishing a bouquet handle*

Classic or shower bouquet

In effect, this is an inverted facing arrangement with all mounting wires being fed into a central tying point.

Method 1   Assemble main part of longest trail, extending the mounting wire and strengthening it by adding more wires in order to counterbalance the weight of all material on the main unit. Establish centre of the design by adding part of the returned end. Then mark the height and volume by inserting the central flower, see figure 52.

Add other units, binding neatly into one central point. Add foliage as the design builds up, either in units or as single leaves, or both.

Method 2   Beginning with the central flower, follow the guidelines for assembling a five-point posy. Begin the trail, attaching it unit by unit to the 'posy', the shorter units first, then the longer ones until the full length of the design is established. This method is the complete reverse of method 1. It is convenient if working with very delicate and expensive flowers sometimes used at the edges of a design, for example, lily-of-the-valley. If the 'framework' of the bouquet, as in method 1, is described with very

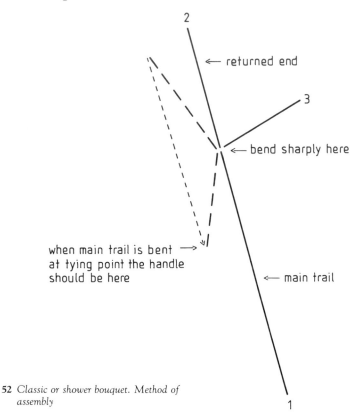

2

← returned end

3

← bend sharply here

when main trail is bent →
at tying point the handle
should be here

← main trail

52 *Classic or shower bouquet. Method of
assembly*

1

delicate material first, it will be vulnerable to accidental damage while the rest of the material is being inserted.

Method 3   The design is assembled in two parts: first the centre and top part, as in method 2. Next build the trail. Then join the two sections together very firmly at the binding point.

Semi-crescent design
The proportions for this elegant type of bouquet are approximately the same as for the classic design, that is, one-third to two-thirds, see figure 53.

The curve can be either to the left or to the right, but when designing for two or four bridesmaids, who will be walking side by side, make each bouquet a near-mirror image of the other, curving one to the right, the other to the left. Make the curve emphatic both of the returned end and the trail. That is to say, it must not look like a classic bouquet that has somehow been pushed slightly out of shape.

Method of assembly Gradually build the shape as each piece of material is added. This will ensure good balance. You should be aware of the 'feel' of the design through the hand that is holding it as it is assembled. As both the main trail and the returned end are curving in the same direction, the bouquet might tend to tilt. This can be corrected by adding a little more material away from the curve and also by gently bending all units out from the centre. This has the effect of re-deploying the weight into the handle. Figure 53.

Full crescent bouquet
This is similar to the shape of a bascade or baskette. It is, in effect, the equivalent of almost two semi-crescent designs and is, consequently, extravagant in materials.

Method Divide the material into two parts. Each side of the design need not be identical, but it is easier to judge quantities when each side is seen separately. Also prepare several units to form the centre.

Assemble about two-thirds of one of the main trails. Build a second one from the second section of material, but containing a little less material. Check for length against the first trail.

The most important factor is that these two main trails shall be bound together at the centre of the design and that they stay in position. This is the main reason for not taping too much material on to one 'backbone' or mounting wire. Having decided on the centre of the bouquet, ie, the length of each main trail, place the two terminal flowers together so that the trails lie against each other. Then bind the mounting wires firmly together beginning at the centre, bind to the end and up again. This should prevent the trails from twisting.

Bend each trail outwards from the centre at the angle that is wanted and check that they stay in place. If either seems insecure, cut the binding and begin again, for if these first trails are not firm, the bouquet will never stay in shape.

In conclusion the full crescent design is a fascinating exercise in balance and counterbalance. Decide how many flowers and units can be assembled into the main trail. This will be dictated by the actual weight of the flowers and the ultimate spread of the design.

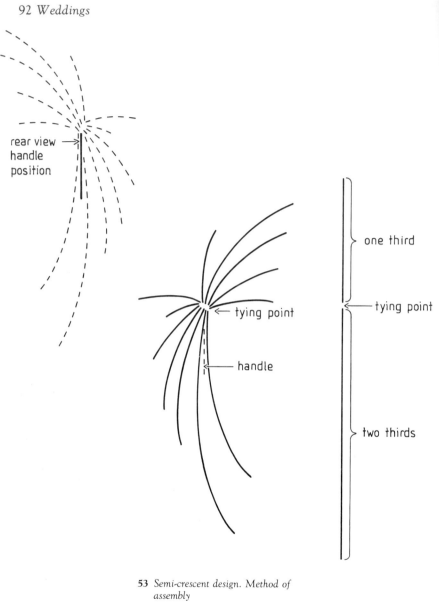

rear view →
handle
position

← tying point

handle

one third

← tying point

two thirds

53 *Semi-crescent design. Method of assembly*

54 *Semi-crescent design*

Therefore there can be more lightweight flowers on one unit and fewer heavy ones. Roses, in particular, are surprisingly weighty and more than two blooms on one unit are inclined to drag. It follows then, that the mount wire for each unit passes through the tying point to the bouquet handle. The weight is counterbalanced in the hand and does not pull from the centre of the bouquet.

Bascade or baskette

This is really a full crescent on a smaller scale, but with a handle. It is a most versatile design, for it can be made to almost any size and is particularly charming for very small bridesmaids. However, it is difficult to assemble and students should try each of the methods suggested to decide which one works the best.

Prepare two corsage-type designs, building unit to unit and trimming away excess wire wherever suitable. This is so that the joining point shall be as slender as possible.

Method 1 Cut the remaining mount wires of one side to about 8 cm long. Elongate the second one, taping in extra wires, so that it will form the major portion of the handle, probably between 12 and 20 cm. Therefore the wire must be extended to twice this length.

Add some strips of *Kleenex* tissue to the longer portion of the handle if you think it ought to be a little fatter. Tape both parts of handle, then gently bend the longer section to form handle shape.

Place both designs very close together, their bases touching, so that the longer section of handle crosses the shorter section. Bind very securely with a taped wire .56 (24). The join may have to be pinched together with a small pair of pliers. Complete the handle curve so that the two ends overlap (this should be in amongst the central flowers). Bind the join securely with silver wire and tape over, see figure 55.

Cover the handle with ribbon. A multi-loop bow can be added to mask the join.

Method 2 Prepare a handle by taping wires together to the required length and thickness. Cover with ribbon, leaving the two wire ends uncovered 2 to 3 cm. Shape the wire to form the handle, figure 56. Bend the tips of the wire (the uncovered 2 cm) sharply at right-angles to the handle, inwards so that they overlap. Bind these two wires together very firmly and tape over. This small

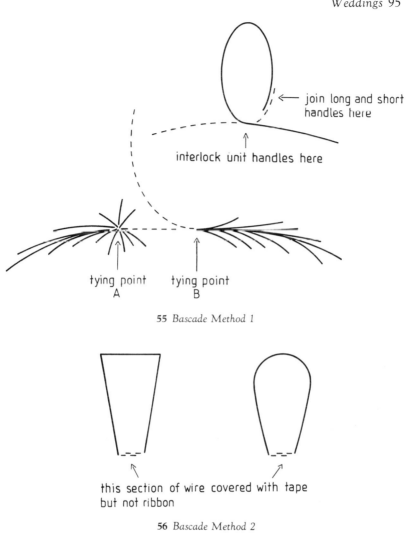

55 *Bascade Method 1*

56 *Bascade Method 2*

section of taped wire forms the anchoring spot for the two flower units.

Method 3   Prepare the handle as for method 2. Assemble most of the two units and bind them with silver wire to the base of the handle. Insert the rest of the central material (whether single flowers and/or small units), holding the mounting wires firmly together in one hand, as if assembling a bouquet.

This will form a small handle below the centre of the design. Trim it off as short as possible, approximately 4 cm, tape and mask with ribbon loops.

Open posy

This can be made either with single whole flowers and foliage, or with smaller material built into units. If whole flowers are used, each stem should reach the centre of the posy, the tying point, but should not extend below for it is far easier to bind a taped wire than a wired stem. Figure 57.

The design is assembled on the five-point basis. Each set of five inserts should be the same length. The spread of the first set of five will determine the size of the posy. Position the centre so that the final outline is a gentle curve.

57 *Components of open posy*

Finishing without a posy frill   Edge the posy with foliage or tulle. Place a figure of eight bow on wire .70 or .56 (22 or 24) at the back of the design. Add more ribbon loops and trails to the front if required. Tape firmly and then finish handle with ribbon.

58 *Open posy*

Finishing with posy frill Insert handle and ease the frill up as high as possible to the top of the handle, so that it encircles the first set of inserts. Add backing bow and ribbon loops, then finish handle with ribbon. Figure 58.

Duchesse or Carmen rose

This is assembled from the outer petals of at least ten well-conditioned open flowers. Wire the petals in pairs, for greater textural strength, with silver .38 or .46 (28 or 26). Mount if necessary, as for the Victorian posy. Choose a neat bud for the central flower. Follow the same method of assembly as for the Victorian posy (sometimes known as a *Colonial posy* or *tuzzy-muzzy*). Continue feeding in each layer until the required size is achieved. Edge with foliage and trim with ribbon.

A smaller version of this rose posy makes a very attractive lapel spray, handbag ornament or, lavishly trimmed with tulle, could be worn as a wedding hat.

Any petals or foliage that tolerate being wired can be used for this design. Tulip petals look very attractive but do not usually last as long as roses. An extremely long-lasting posy can be made with leaves of eucalyptus populus, which will gradually dry and remain decorative for several months.

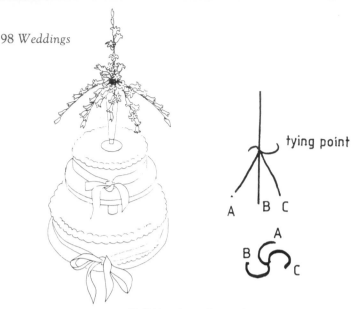

tying point

59 *Bride cake top in container*

Bride cake top

In container This is assembled on the five-point basis, but usually with an extra tall centre. The units or single flowers (wired and taped) are built into one 'stem' into the hand, the central tying point being bound with silver wire. Add several multi-loop bows of narrow ribbon, see figure 59. Measure the size of the handle with the container, both for width and length, for the design should fit firmly into the vase so that the binding point is fractionally below the rim and the five trails curve gracefully over the edge. If the handle has to be enlarged to fit, overbind with *Kleenex* tissue, tape and finish with ribbon.

Without a container Assemble as a five-point posy, cutting away as much excess wire as possible, so that the final binding point is neat and slender. Figure 59.

Divide the wires below the binding point into three equal parts. Cut them to about 3 cm and bind with tape. Carefully bind each small 'leg' with narrow ribbon, beginning at the tip and binding towards the design. Secure the ribbon with *Sellotape*. Carefully curve each leg so that the three of them together form a base for the design.

NOTE They must be curved sideways for the design should seem to rest on the cake. The binding point and support legs must not be visible.

Victorian posy

This is composed of rings of small flowers, florets or other suitable material built evenly around a central bud or flower. The finished effect is charming, but they consume a good deal of time and material. Each ring should be of one colour; this can, of course, be repeated but only after several other circles have been inserted.

Method   Wire the material, taping it to about 2 cm only. It can then be mounted, in pairs, to a slightly heavier wire .56 (24). Again tape sparingly for this will all be hidden in the handle and too much build-up of tape will make it too thick.

Cut the stem of the central flower to about 3 cm. Wire the flower internally if possible and tape. Bind in the first ring of flowers, so that they are only just below the level of the central flower, for the finished effect should be a shallow elipse, reminiscent of the shape of a dahlia. Continue inserting each successive ring of material, binding as close to the first binding point as possible. Thus, the support wires of each ring will be longer than the previous ones until the outside ring is set almost at right-angles to the main stem, see figure 60. Finish edge with a frill or foliage, or both.

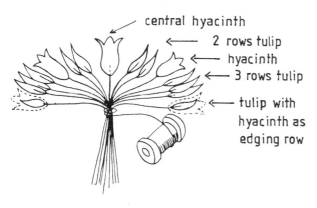

central hyacinth

← 2 rows tulip

← hyacinth

← 3 rows tulip

← tulip with hyacinth as edging row

60 *Victorian posy. Method of assembly*

61 *Pomander*

Pomander (flower ball)

Prepare a multi-loop bow with one small loop, then a large one, then another small one to match the first.

Tape the centre 4 cm of a .70 (22) wire. Pass it through the centre of the large loop, double the wire and twist once. Drive both wires through the middle of a dry foam sphere and return ends back into the foam.

NOTE This means the foam that is used for everlasting arrangements, not the foam that is soaked. Have no fear, the flowers last surprisingly well.

The large loop forms the handle which should now be firmly in place. Insert prepared material at the base, working towards the handle. Any small flowers that last well may be used, but remember that the circumference of the design will increase in relation to twice the depth of the flowers. Hyacinths are ideal for this design, but as each floret is about 2 cm long, it may be necessary to trim the ball down before beginning work.

Delicate flowers that are normally supported with a silver .46 (26) or even a lighter wire, can be fixed into the foam with a straight pin (a dressmaker's pin). The shaft of the pins should be as long as possible so that they drive well into the foam. A floral ball is very attractive even without any extra adornment. However, one can add a corsage if desired. Pin it securely at the top, so that the fixing is hidden under the loops. Finally add ribbon to the base of the pomander, making certain that the loops are inserted directly in line with the handle loop. Figure 61.

Outside decorations

Artistically speaking, these are generally very rewarding for the designer. It is a chance to work sometimes 'larger than life', to use materials that are not usually in current use and to work away from the bench in a different environment. The magnitude or otherwise of the arrangements will no doubt have been decided at point of sale. Always try to arrive at a clear understanding with the client as to what is expected. If you are working within a rather modest budget, explain that one lavish design will carry far more impact than several smaller ones, particularly for church or hall decoration. People standing in groups, maybe at a party or wedding reception, tend to obscure designs that are positioned on tables, window sills or a pedestal. It is a disappointment if only the top few flowers can be glimpsed above the heads of the guests so the type of occasion will, to a certain extent, guide the plans.

Therefore, try to site designs at least above shoulder-height. This might mean that it is not feasible to use any conventional containers. If the decoration is for the one occasion only, the flowers will be perfectly all right in soaked foam bases. They must, of course, be crisp and firm but showing plenty of colour.

Church arrangements

Whatever the occasion, most likely a wedding, possibly a christening and sometimes a funeral, it is advisable to contact the incumbent or the verger, or whoever is in charge of keys, well in advance. Nowadays many churches are kept locked, so the first point is to arrange a time of access which must, obviously, also be when no other ceremony is being conducted.

You may already know the church well, in which case these preliminaries are unnecessary. However, have a sketch plan ready so that you can indicate the approximate size of the designs and where you would like to put them. Fortunately most churches appreciate having more flowers than usual to beautify the interior. On the other hand, there are some areas where flowers are not permitted (on the altar in some instances) so it is just as well to check on all this before finalising your plans.

It must be agreed, too, not only with your client, but also with the church, which designs are to be left and which removed after the ceremony. For example, pedestal designs and arrangements set in most of the 'usual' places will definitely be left, but if there are pew sprays or any other kind of aisle decoration such as flower trees with ropes of smilax between, then these obviously cannot be left without agreement with the authorities. The font may be specially decorated for a christening and it is possible that these arrangements might have to be removed.

All these details will affect your final estimate for it involves extra work, extra mileage and extra time.

To make pew spray decorations   These can be made in the workroom on the basis of a facing arrangement with a shorter main vertical. Bear in mind these designs will be seen from above so take a little extra material in case the top requires more furnishing.

Method

1   Spray the polystyrene base with dark green *Oasis-spray*

2   See figure 62. Curve heavy-gauge wire about the weight of a wire coat hanger. Drive the two ends firmly into the base

3   Mask the soaked foam and make the design, taking care not to make the centre too high for this will project into the aisle and the flowers may get damaged as people pass

4   Suspend the designs where the foam can drain out but not dehydrate. Take some newspaper to protect the base of each pew in case the designs are still shedding water. They will not drop for very long and by the time all the work has been completed, it should be possible to gather up the newspaper

5   Add ribbon bows either at the top of the pew or at the base of the design

How to attach to a traditional pew

1   Fix small strips of draught-excluder to the top of the pew so that the wire does not damage the wood

2   Curve the wire over the top of the pew, resting on the draught-excluder. Make sure that there is sufficient wire to counterbalance the pull of the design

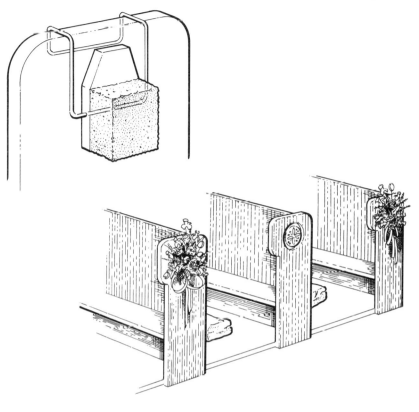

62 *Pew spray decorations*

3   If extra security is required the back of the design can be
supported against the pew-end with a generous piece of *Oasis-fix*.
Put some tape on the spot first, then attach the fixative, otherwise
it may leave a stain on the wood.

If sprays are required in a church that has chairs instead of the
traditional pews, the foam base should be considerably smaller.
Bind tape around the spot where you plan to fix the design and
then attach with strong binding wire. Unless the client insists, this
type of design is not very suitable for, apart from the technical
problems, no one would be able to sit on the chair. An alternative
would be flower spheres attached to the top of poles which can be
attached to the chair with wire. A white bow is arranged over the
join.

Flower spheres Decide how high you want the finished designs (they should be a minimum of 2.5 m from the ground). Broomhandles or dowelling should be painted either white or gold. Soaked foam is attached to the top of the pole. There are several ways this can be done, the following is both simple and secure:

1 Drive a long nail right through the pole about 4 cm below the top. Trim the top of the pole so that it is less fat and solid. Do not trim too sharply otherwise the nail may split the wood.

2 Very gently impale the foam on the pole, easing it down until it almost rests on the arms of the large nail. Cover the foam block with wire mesh and fix securely with wire to the nail. The size of the foam must be determined by the amount of flowers to be used, also the size of their stems. It may be necessary to add moss before the mesh, but bear in mind that this will increase the size of the foam base.

3 Insert a little masking foliage. Flowers are arranged using an extension of the all-round technique. Cut six stems the same length. Insert one on top, one underneath and one either side. That is, four stems marking the extremities of the 'equator' of the sphere or globe, and one north, the other south. Work within these markers, adding more flowers, some with very short stems to recess, others with longer stems (as for the open posy), but none should be longer than the first six markers.

Flower trees are made on the same basis, except that the poles must be anchored into a base very firmly. This could be damp sand – make sure your container is strong enough to hold the weight – or a semi-permanent base can be prepared with cement.

Method This obviously also requires a very strong container. Partly fill with cement and insert the pole. It can be removed when the cement is firm for easier transportation, if necessary. It is also easier to arrange the flowers at the top of the pole when it is not in place.

Having made this arrangement, set the pole back into the hole in the cement and fix a block of soaked foam either one side, or both sides of the pole. Make a design to furnish the base of the pole with flowers and foliage or with foliage alone. Figure 63.

These flower 'trees' have a multitude of uses; to decorate a large church or cathedral; a patio for a summer party; they could, in

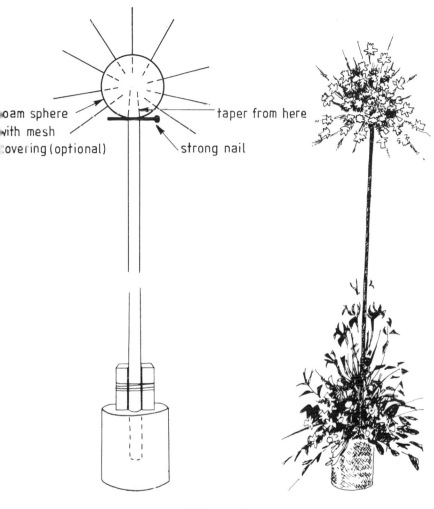

oam sphere
vith mesh
:overing (optional)

taper from here

strong nail

63 *Flower spheres*

calm weather, be used to line the pathway up to the church or as marquee decoration.

They can be made to almost any dimension and look enchanting as table designs about 90 cm high. Smaller ones need not, of course, be based in cement; they can be anchored in ornamental pots or ordinary flower pots. A closely-packed holly 'tree' is very decorative, particularly if the support is painted dark green. Not only are these designs adaptable for many social occasions, they are useful for shop display and window decoration.

Working on location Each florist must be responsible for his or her own tools. Make a checklist of other necessities and keep it pinned on the noticeboard. It should include plastic sheeting, a watering can, sprayer, all the various design tackle such as spare wires, tape, possibly a small hammer and nails, gimlet, screwdriver and pliers, broom, brush and dustpan, dry dusters (in quantity) and small first aid kit. Designers must reckon to be completely self-contained down to the last detail, which should include rubbish sacks, refreshment for snacks and small change in case a telephone call is necessary. Pen and notebook is also essential. It may be necessary to have soft shoes when working on carpets. And as a final addition to the designer's tool kit, an extending ladder may sometimes be essential!

10 Window dressing and display

Objectives

Your shop window plays an extremely important part in establishing and maintaining your business image. Basically, putting merchandise in the shop window is one way of indicating that you are in business. It is also a way of showing the class and type of goods on offer. However, this is a very elementary concept of window dressing and florists naturally aim at something more sophisticated.

The flower industry is one of the few areas, pehaps the only one, where its members buy the raw materials (flowers, plants and foliage), take them back to base and condition them ready for processing into the finished product (arrangements, etc). Many other products are pre-packed, and are not only delivered to the store, but a representative from the particular organisation can usually be seen arranging said product on the shelves. In the world of cosmetics, the retailer's window can be dressed by one firm for a given time, then another takes its place.

Window dressing is a technique in itself and, as well as the circumstances previously mentioned, all large stores have their own resident dressers, and very highly-qualified they are.

So far as I know, no such service exists for the flower industry. Window dressing with perishable merchandise would only be valid for a day or so. But now that everlasting (silk and polyester) flowers, foliage and plants are here to stay, as well as dried materials, I foresee a whole new service area for trained people with a special liking for being 'on the road'. One would need constantly to be on the move, travelling from one shop to the next, gradually building up a chain of clients, thus releasing the busy florist to attend to other facets of the business.

Meanwhile, as florists, we need to comprehend the purpose of

64 *Attractive shop display*

window dressing and display beyond the very basic fact of putting goods in the window.

The dictionary defines window dressing as 'the art of arranging goods attractively'. A straightforward, cut-and-dried definition. The word *display* goes several steps further: 'to show ostentatiously, or to exhibit with a view to calling attention' which is precisely what the florist hopes to do. So the main functions of a window display can be itemised as:

1 To appeal to the public, all of whom should be regarded as potential customers
2 To command attention
3 To capture the imagination
4 To convince the potential customer of the necessity to buy

Certain commodities are regarded as basic necessities and the public has, albeit subconsciously, a built-in purchase impulse. Most people accept the fact that, from time to time they need to buy soap and walking shoes, toothpaste and potatoes. Flowers, however, are still regarded by some people as special occasion items, so the initial impulse must come from the vendor.

It is a mistaken premise to imagine that flowers sell themselves. True, they have tremendous appeal, but the arresting window display that means action on both sides of the counter must be something considerably more than neat containers full of fresh flowers.

This type of window dressing – no stretch of the imagination could call it display – will carry absolutely no impact or persuasion. The public needs to identify with the display, so that the reaction is not a casual 'how pretty,' or 'that's nice,' but 'I like – I want – I must buy'. The public has been appealed to, attention has been arrested and the imagination captured. Conviction of the necessity to buy follows, which forms the ideal progression.

Therefore a good window display should at least invoke the first two reactions, namely, looking and wanting. Even if the decision to purchase does not follow, display is never wasted. Your shop window, like your delivery vehicle, forges a continuous link between your organisation and your public. One florist in Germany even uses his truck for a moving display: the vehicle has glass windows each side and at the back. Mounted on pieces of wood he has designed beautiful montages of dried materials. These 'pictures' hook on inside the windows. He has made several such designs which can be changed according to the season.

To sum up in general terms: window display is, obviously, a form of advertising. Nobody expects 100 per cent positive results from an advertisement, nor can it be assumed that everyone that admires the flower shop window will immediately become a customer. It is, however, reasonable to hope that a large percentage of the public will eventually become buyers by virtue of the strength of appeal of your window display.

Practical basics
Meaningful window dressing should follow the same concepts as those applied generally throughout the shop. Namely, everything should be clean, neat, good quality and taste. Flowers and plants will be of the highest quality; containers, stands and accessories all should be clean and fresh in appearance.

Price tickets
This is a much-discussed subject amongst florists. It has been heard time and time again that some people are loath to go into a flower shop because nothing is priced. Fair comment, and there is

no doubt that price display is essential in the build-up of customer-confidence. Look in other shop windows. Even if you never intend to buy a mink coat or a grand piano, it is still interesting to see the price clearly displayed. Study shop window display whenever you can; in most instances the merchandise is discreetly priced. Flowers should be no exception.

Each ticket should be clear and fresh-looking; no larger than is necessary for it to be read easily by passers-by. Fix a price list in one corner of the window, indicating flowers and plants currently available. This means that not every single item on display need be priced for the public will have a good general idea of your price-range from this list.

All accessories such as containers and ornaments will have been priced before they are put on display. Use small adhesive tickets that can be fixed to the base of the article. Some florists also attach a gold label carrying their name and telephone number to every piece of merchandise. This is all on-going advertising which ultimately adds up to more business.

Guidelines

One's approach to planning a window display should be much the same as when making an arrangement. The ingredients are still colour, shape and size of material; use recession and repetition to achieve your impact. Treat the whole window like a picture frame with depth, using space so that the eye can travel comfortably from one area to the next. The alternative to a window display could, of course, be to emphasise one special design, an interesting plant or even a very special container with just one flower. A dark backdrop is essential here so that the window appears smaller. This is a very useful ploy when time is short.

Encourage every member of staff to take an interest in display, for ideas pooled are always helpful. It is certainly not logical to assume that only senior members of staff should be responsible for display. As florists, we aim to appeal to every age group, so obviously we need ideas fed in from people of all ages.

Special displays

Some seasons are absolute 'naturals' for window display; for example, Christmas, St Valentine's Day, Mother' Day and Easter, yet there are many other occasions that could be highlighted.

Keep in touch with local happenings so that, say, a school concert, a play at a local theatre, almost anything at all that is pleasantly newsworthy can be emphasised with a particular flower or plant display. Ask your travel agent for posters which invoke sunshine, warmth and colour. Display a different one from time to time with appropriate flowers and accessories.

Or adopt, perhaps, a particular element as basis for your display: maybe wood, together with green plants. Another time invoke an ethereal atmosphere by using glass – containers, baubles and columns faced with mirror glass from the local DIY store. Complement it with delicate arrangements of one colour. The possibilities are endless.

Lighting

Display naturally involves a certain amount of lighting, even during the daytime. The strength used will, to a certain extent, be governed by the shop location, the prevailing weather and general external light value. But never be sparing with light, either in the window or shop, for a poorly-lit shop creates a very bad impression. Conversely, the florist has to take into consideration the fact that light creates heat, which can be detrimental to flowers. Remember that roses, tulips and anemones, particularly, react very quickly to light and they should not be exposed in the window in direct light, either from overhead or bright sunshine. The heat generated by display lighting builds up considerably once the shop is closed. For this reason always remove susceptible flowers and keep them stored in the dark.

But this is certainly not sufficient reason for never having the window illuminated during the evening or at weekends. An unlighted window is doing nothing, absolutely nothing, to enhance your public image. An attractive display, properly lighted, is working for you all the time. If a time switch is fitted, to control the lighting from closing time until, say, midnight, plus Sundays, the display time adds up to at least forty hours a week. This is forty more hours when your display could be working for you. Evening and weekend lighting can be minimised to one spotlight. In fact, this gives a more dramatic effect as opposed to the highly-illuminated overall effect of daytime lighting. And it does not necessarily, have to be the window itself that is highlighted. Sometimes try the effect of concentrating the spotlight on another subject within the shop. The effect here, also, is very dramatic and usually makes the shop look far larger than it really is.

Designs
As well as cut flowers and plants, it is vital that designs are also displayed, both in the window and as an important part of the interior shop display. This is an area in which fabric flowers and foliage can be very useful, but take care not to leave any particular arrangements on display for too long.

The public is conditioned to buying by seeing and things not on show are unlikely to sell. In other words, people rarely ask for an arrangement unless they see one or two examples. Moreover, even one or two simple designs with some flowers in season will help customers to identify the cut flowers also displayed in relation to their own homes or possibly as gifts.

Any designs displayed should be clearly priced. And why not give each a name, so that people can readily describe any particular arrangement, not by saying 'the one that had three gladioli, five carnations, some fuzzy white stuff and a large ribbon bow', but by its name. Here are a few suggestions and no doubt, you can add many more – 'Forever Yours'; 'Easter Dawn'; 'Swan Lake'; 'Midsummer Madness'. Giving the design a name implies that it is special and this should increase its sales appeal. Good wine is known by name – why not good flower design?

Whatever the dimensions of the window, never forget that an attractive display will, by and large, carry far more impact than a series of newspaper advertisements, though, obviously, advertising is also essential in our present-day business climate.

Window shopping
Most people enjoy 'window shopping' and your weekend and evening display may generate more business than you ever thought possible. However, on very busy days it may be difficult to keep the display up to standard, though your minimum aim should be simply to see that it is tidy and clean. At other times, the sky's the limit for imagination and initiative in display. Your window is your silent publicity officer; make sure he works in your favour.

11 Care and conditioning of perishable stock

You are doubtless wondering why such a basic operation as conditioning the flowers was not included in one of the first chapters.

Flowers and foliage – our day-to-day stock – is an expensive item. Good quality material is vital to our work output; it is imperative that the florist has whatever is required for any particular design. As an example, an order for a table centrepiece in specific colours for a dinner party the same evening would be a disaster if all bud flowers were used, showing little or no colour. Alternatively, a client buying cut flowers for the home usually wants maximum vase life from the purchase. So conditioning is not just a question of unpacking market boxes, cutting stem ends and putting everything in water.

Care of existing stock and conditioning the incoming materials is a very specialised and exciting area of the florist's work. Flowers now come from all over the globe; they may have been in transit for several days. Anyone who has suffered the slightest jet-lag will understand the longing for rest and a cool drink. Flowers are not very different from people in this respect; some travel better than others, but treated with care and understanding, they expand and grow to make glorious and colourful displays in our shops.

The time of year, source of origin, daily weather conditions, as well as the purpose for which the flower is required; all these factors have relevant bearing on how stock should be treated. Thus, this particular daily operation should be under the supervision of an experienced florist and it must be made clear to students that treatment suitable for one time of the year may not be correct for all time.

Care of stock, general

This includes routine tidying, checking all flowers for their potential vase life, sorting out saleable and usable material and, of course, discarding the remainder. This carries quite a weight of responsibility, for the profit margin can be materially affected by waste. An even more solemn thought is that the business image can also be seriously affected by bad judgment regarding potential vase life, flower quality and general care of existing stock.

Cut flowers

In most instances, the public quite logically expects cut flowers to offer maximum vase life. This means that, after purchase, they will gradually expand to full maturity. They should, therefore, be sold before reaching this stage, as cut flowers, that is. However, they mature at different speeds and in different conditions, so it is almost impossible to apply a rigid set of rules. Experience in handling and knowing the source of supply does help. Here the operative word is *experience*, for rules can be learnt, but experience has to be built up gradually over the years. It is certainly no loss of face, therefore, for any student-florist to lack experience, for this precious commodity will surely come in time.

Maturity Some flowers show their age more quickly and decisively than others. For example, tulips and roses leave very little doubt as to their condition at any stage of development. On the other hand, carnations, chrysanthemums and orchids have a relatively long period of maturity and it is sometimes baffling for inexperienced staff to perceive what stage the flower has reached.

Suffice it to say that only flowers with maximum potential vase life should be sold or packed for gift bouquets. More mature blooms, even so, have their uses in the scheme of things, for flowers with maximum colour visible are ideal for most funeral designs as well as for shop display.

Stock conditioning, general

* Prepare suitable containers with flower preservative solution. Few flowers require more than 10 cm of water.
* Remove leaves from lower part of stems.
* Cut small piece off stem end with a sharp, sloping cut, thus encouraging the flower to drink. This will obviously hasten maturity of the flower. Therefore, in certain instances it is advisable not to cut the stem end.

* Always cut with a sharp knife, *not* scissors, which tend to constrict the stem ends and may inhibit the flower taking up water.

Special subjects

Chrysanthemums Both spray and standard blooms will take up water more readily if the stems are broken by hand, not cut. Figure 65. Do not crush or hammer. This results in an untidy end which quickly pollutes the water.

Poinsettias Cut stem ends and stand in warm flower preservative solution. Store well away from any source of draught, protecting the blooms with an overwrap of soft paper, if necessary. Handle these beautiful flowers very carefully for if a leaf is accidentally broken from the stem, latex will flow out.

Euphorbia Since this belongs to the same family as poinsettia, it is not surprising that it should receive the same conditioning treatment. Some designers like to defoliate completely each stem so that the small clusters of flowers show up to better advantage. This should be done carefully but quickly, taking care that the latex does not disfigure the flowers.

Gerberas Cut stem ends and stand in deep containers in warm flower preservative solution to a depth of 8 to 10 cm. The purpose of the deep container is that the stems will be well supported while they are taking up water. Store in a temperature of not less than 15°C and away from all draughts. Gerberas may require several days to become properly conditioned. If they are to be used for decoration, it is best to wire them internally before conditioning. It is far easier to insert a wire through a straight stem before it has taken up water, for gerberas sometimes curve as they drink. These curves can, of course, be used to great advantage in arrangements, but a gentle support wire gives the florist greater control.

Lily-of-the-valley (Convalleria) The forced variety is marketed in bundles of ten stems, together with its own pale green foliage, still on the root ball. This flower now is used almost exclusively for bridal work and should always be wired *before* it is conditioned. See chapter on wiring.

If you have a garden, plant the root ball in a shady spot; it may grow and naturalise.

65 *Breaking chrysanthemum stems by hand*

The outdoor variety has a regrettably short flowering season, but is particularly prized for its delicate perfume. Condition it in shallow water (6 cm) but use a fairly deep container so that the fragile bunches are sheltered from draughts. The flowers also appreciate an overhead spray.

Roses These are possibly the most challenging of this special subjects group for they react differently according to the season, to the source of supply and even according to different varieties. Flowers destined for direct sale should all be de-thorned before being conditioned.

De-thorning means removing all the thorns from each stem. This can be a tedious job; a sharp knife, time and patience is all that is needed. Hold the knife parallel to the stem and strip thorns and foliage from the lower 10 cm (Figure 66.) Do not damage the stem as each thorn is stripped away. Some people prefer to use scissors, which are valid, but not nearly so rapid. Holding this cleared piece of stem in one hand, work upwards towards the bloom, stripping off thorns and carefully avoiding the rest of the foliage. Remember to keep the blade of the knife flat so that only the thorn is cut.

Stephanotis This is another flower that is used almost exclusively for bridal work. It does not require conditioning in the accepted sense of the word. It is usually packed for market in polythene bags. Wire each floret, straight from the bag, tape it and, if possible, build it into units (see chapter on wiring). Then spray well and store in polythene bags or boxes.

Dahlias These will drink more readily if most of the foliage is removed. Cut the stem ends and condition in shallow water. The continued emphasis on shallow water may confuse people who have been in the habit of putting all flowers into the deepest possible water. But as the result of extensive research, it is now apparent that flowers take up water just as readily when stood in shallow water. Naturally the water level should be checked from time to time, particularly when conditioning fast-drinking flowers like gladioli.

Bulb-grown flowers The majority take up water very easily. If the weather is warm and bright, it may not even be necessary to cut the stem ends of daffodils, narcissi, iris, tulips, anemones

66 Stripping thorns from rose stems

and freesia. But the decision whether to cut or not must be the responsibility of an experienced florist. The development of some bulb flowers can sometimes be arrested by standing the bunches in an empty container for not longer than 24 hours. They should then be conditioned in the usual way.

Orchids Many of these are surprisingly tough, long-lasting flowers. All the same, they should be treated with care for some varieties bruise easily, while others could have parts of the flower snapped off with thoughtless handling. The most popular varieties in use in the flower shop are cymbidium, cattleyas, phalaenopsis and dendrobium. The first two are very crisp; cattleyas, in particular, are very large and opulent in appearance. Odontoglossums are usually smaller which make them very attractive for special corsages. With the exception of cattleyas, which are generally sold individually, the other varieties can either be bought on the stem – or separately according to the policy of the supply source.

Condition the stems as usual, that is, cut with a sharp knife and stand in flower preservative solution. To condition a single orchid on a short stem, first prepare a small container full of water and spread some white paper tightly over the top, securing it with a rubber band. Pierce a hole in the paper and gently put the flower stem through the hole so that the bloom is resting on the paper and the stem is in the water. Do not store orchids in a cooling cabinet.

Singapore orchids are usually despatched from source with each stem in a tiny phial of water. There are five or ten stems in each vacuum pack. To condition these long-lasting flowers, submerge the complete stems, flowers and all, in a large receptacle, either sink or bath, for several hours. Then cut the stem ends, as usual, and stand them in flower preservative solution.

Foliages
Many foliages in commercial use have woody stems that should be broken or else cut with a sharp knife. Then condition in warm or cool water, depending on the time of year. Generally speaking, flowers and foliage take up water more readily in warmer weather. In cold weather, some flowers arrive actually looking cold as well as being cold to the touch. The florist instinctively knows that these flowers will be happier in warm to hot water – never boiling,

please. Foliage such as cupressus, laurel and holly need not be conditioned providing it can be stored out of doors (covered in extreme weather) or in an outhouse.

Decorative foliage such as hosta, croton, wild arum should be totally submerged in cool water for several hours, after which treatment it lasts wonderfully well.

Dry pack

Dry pack is the term that indicates flowers and foliage that have been packed and despatched immediately after harvesting without an initial plunge into water. This technique is on the increase for the consignment does not weigh as much as flowers containing water. Consequently more stems can be packed in each box. Moreover they are less vulnerable to damage in transit, being completely limp and consequently presenting little resistance to pressure. They need, however, about one day longer to condition thoroughly. When buying dry pack, do not be confused by the apparently half-dead appearance of both flowers and foliage. Condition them as usual, standing in flower preservative solution. Store them in an even temperature of not less than 12.8°C. They will soon expand and in a day or so should be indistinguishable from material treated in the traditional manner.

Cool storage

This type of storage is used by growers and wholesalers, while an increasing number of florists are also having coolers installed. Coolers, though, are definitely not refrigerators such as are used for storage of perishable foods. Domestic refrigerators, also, are unsuitable for flower storage.

There are a number of specialist firms who will give advice on which model to have, as well as making the installation. There is absolutely no doubt that they do prove a boon to the florist, but, like any other appliance, need to be understood so as to enjoy maximum benefit.

Flowering and foliage plants

These are also an integral part of the florist's stock. They should receive almost as much care and attention as the cut flowers for an appealing range of healthy plants contributes a great deal to general display.

Positioning   Except for the very largest specimens, try to group them where they will be seen to advantage but also in a position that suits their demands. Even if the florist is not conversant with every variety there are a number of informative books containing excellent advice. All-in-all, a well-grown healthy plant makes very few demands on the busy florist; most require good light, but not strong sunlight; some are tolerant of less light; none enjoys being in a draught, and the majority require regular watering.

Watering   Rain water is ideal for all plants, but failing this, always keep a full can in the shop so that the water is not stone cold direct from the tap. Plants absorb water at different speeds and those that require very little, eg Sansevieria (Mother-in-law's tongue) should be displayed separately, so that they are not on the receiving end of the general watering round. Most plants dehydrate more rapidly in warm and windy weather.

Grooming   Carefully remove any spent blooms, shrivelled or fading leaves and, of course, never leave a plant standing in water, except on occasion, a very thirsty hydrangea. St Paulias, in particular, happily continue flowering for several months so long as the faded blooms are removed regularly. From time to time clean the foliage of broad-leaved subjects such as ficus elasticus, croton, diffenbachia and aspidistra (which is rapidly returning to favour) with a damp *Kleenex*, using plain water, not oil or milk. After cleaning, burnish with a very light spray of *Leafshine* or similar preparation. The amount of dust, etc, on foliage depends, obviously on the location of the shop. Cleaning may have to be carried out weekly, or twice-weekly or, for a fortunate minority, only once in several weeks.

Deposits on the foliage inhibit respiration. Therefore regular grooming and an occasional shine-up is essential to the plant's well-being as well as to its appearance and consequent saleability.

Display   Group different types of plants so that variations in leaf shape, colour and size complement one another. However, do avoid overcrowding them as this may result in damaged foliage. Any plants used in window display should not be left in the same position for more than a few days. The extra light and heat may 'draw' them unevenly.

Obviously the florist's main objective is to keep a brisk throughput of decorative plants. But if some remain unchosen for it could be that they are either too large, too small or just generally appealing to the public. However, do not condemn the 'rejects' as failures. For with care they will still furnish the shop and will certainly come in handy for decoration work.

Fresh intake of plants   Foliage and flowering plants are usually kept fairly dry for transportation. They should therefore be given generous watering and the pots cleaned where necessary. Every plant must be checked for quality and general appearance. As with all other merchandise, price each one before putting it on display.

Feeding   If any plant remains unsold for several weeks it may benefit from an application of liquid feed. Follow the instructions on the bottle precisely. Never imagine that more feed will produce a healthier plant. On the contrary, the extra dose may result in the poor thing being literally burnt to death.

Advice to customers   There is a number of books over a broad price range on the care and maintenance of plants for the home. Certainly give as much advice as you can at point of sale, but also encourage the customers to invest in a plant book, so that they always have the information handy. One question that is impossible to answer precisely is 'how much water does it need?' For the honest answer is 'it depends – on the heat of the room, the season of the year, where it is placed (hopefully not on a window sill where it receives direct sunlight through glass)'. Suffice it to say that a plant in soil that is damp to the touch does not need water. And overwatering will hasten the collapse of many healthy plants.

When buying a mature plant many clients have an irresistible urge to re-pot it. As a general rule, most plants do not require this extra attention as soon as they get to their new home: maybe after they have finished flowering, or in a year's time. In fact, if a plant is disturbed during its growing and flowering season, it may suffer a severe check, so the general point of sales advice should be to the effect that the plant will appreciate being left quietly to adjust to its new surroundings; to be watered from time to time but not left to paddle in the overspill.

When the plant pot is in an outer container, put a piece of flower foam not more than 2 cm thick in the base. The plant pot will rest on this small block which will also soak up any excess moisture, see figure 67.

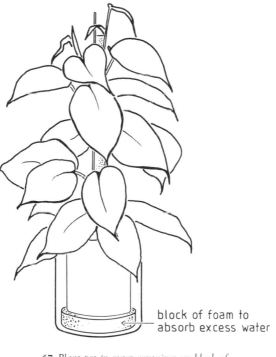

block of foam to
absorb excess water

67 *Plant pot in outer container on block of*
foam

Possible reasons for flowers not taking up water
1 Insufficient or untidy cut. Always use a sharp knife. Scissors, however sharp, tend to constrict the stem cells.

2 Check the stem right up to the flower head to make sure there is no damage, possibly a bend or marking caused by an overtight staking tie in the growing stage.

3 Flower may have been harvested too early. This does sometimes occur with roses, iris, tulips and paeonies. Try a second cut and stand in really hot, not boiling, water. Put in as strong a light as possible.

4 Stem may be stiff yet flower head is limp. Most probably the cause is draught, even that caused by opening and shutting a door continuously, for example, the door into the shop. The flower heads will probably stiffen up as soon as they are removed to a more protected place; meanwhile, wrap them in damp paper until they recover.

5 Sudden head-droop in roses. Still one of the most baffling problems confronting a florist. Sometimes caused by stem damage just under the bloom; possibly draught or both. If no visible damage to the stem, recut stem end and stand in hot water. If the flower head still droops, lay the whole bloom in cool water. Providing the flower was fresh, in most instances it will quickly revive after this treatment. If all else fails, cut the stem much shorter and use the bloom for an arrangement or a buttonhole.

12 Packing and presentation

Research into packing and presentation methods has proved that in respect of those commodities known as *consumer goods* the sales success can be significantly affected by packing and presentation. This does not mean that good presentation ensures long-term sales success for whatever quality merchandise. It does follow, however, that the general public is usually more vulnerable to the purchase-impulse if packaging and presentation are appealing.

Size of package, colour-impact and lettering are all taken into account and there have been instances of a product with a good safe market dropping badly in sales appeal because of an ill-advised change in packaging and presentation.

Challenging thoughts for the florist who is primarily concerned with supplying top-quality flowers and plants. For one is bound to admit the tendency to think that these beautiful natural things have sufficient appeal in themselves and do not need the addition of 'presentation'.

In essence, this is probably true. But looking at it from a different angle, the presentation of any commodity is tangible evidence of the producer's own evaluation of the goods within the package. He wants you to know that his product is ahead of the rest, even before you have sampled it.

Could one apply the same argument to flower packing and presentation? I see no reason why not.

Flowers and food are two of the most perishable commodities to be handled. Food can, however, be deep-frozen and conveniently pre-packed, flowers cannot. True, flowers can be encapsulated in an ice cone and very lovely they look. But once the ice has melted, the flowers are not a bit happy.

Moreover, where deliveries are concerned, the florist serves a very demanding public. Groceries, textiles, furniture, almost anything you can think of, are usually delivered according to a zoning system so that each area receives deliveries, usually on a specific day of the week.

But the florist is concerned, also, with an arbitrary time-factor that must be respected. For no bride would appreciate being told that deliveries to her area took place two days after her wedding: or that, for example, funeral designs could only be delivered after 16.00 hours (4 pm) on three days per week!

Many firms dealing in consumer goods can stockpile their deliveries; they have a special department whose sole responsibility is to prepare the goods for transportation. Some require special gift-wrapping, others only need protection against handling and transport hazards. Either way, it is a job for the expert.

But the florist is coping with deliveries within the daily routine of the shop. The finished article must be produced at the right time, properly prepared for transport, frequently in inclement weather. Without doubt this is also a job for the expert, with usually a tight time schedule just to make things even more difficult.

Cut flower packing

In practice a box is generally the most satisfactory for delivering cut flowers. The contents are well-protected against handling and weather, and the presentation can be varied from the business-like cut flower order package to the most elaborate of gift presentation. A white box needs no paper over-wrap and actually takes less time to prepare than a paper wrap with the same amount of flowers. At peak pressure times, stems can be slipped into a polythene bag and then heavily sprayed; or they can be encased in soaked tissue paper. The boxes can be packed hours before delivery and the contents will still be fresh on arrival. This is certainly not possible with either the regular paper wrap or even the cellophane-fronted bag.

Cellophane presentations A bouquet under cellophane looks extremely festive; indeed, any merchandise that is cellophane-wrapped seems to assume an added value. And when it is finished with a lavish bow the illusion is complete. For there is no doubt that good-quality ribbon contributes a great deal of impact to a flower gift. However, if you use ribbon, use it generously, for a mean bow looks worse than no ribbon at all. Conversely never drown a design with ribbon.

Ribbon finishing   The quickest and simplest way of producing a lavish bow is to use ribbon that was first produced in Italy. There is a matching thin strip of the same ribbon running through which acts as a draw-string, pulling the ribbon up into even-sized loops. In polypropylene, there is a wide choice of colours and it is obtainable from the majority of good wholesalers throughout Britian.

Multi-loop bow   This lavish bow is, admittedly, rather extravagant with ribbon, but it is both versatile and very effective. To make sure that nothing is wasted, always style ribbon bows directly from the bolt, rather than by cutting off a strip which may or may not be accurate in length.

The most important aspect of making this bow neatly is to make sure that the fine silver wire binding is always in the same place. With the running end (bolt of ribbon) away from you, make one loop and bind it tightly several times with the wire. Do not crease this loop, but stretch it sideways by putting two fingers or finger and thumb inside the loop and pushing gently. Then pull the running end quite firmly so that there is no 'slack' at the binding point. Make a second loop and bind once only, both around the second loop and the original. Repeat this until there are sufficient loops, making sure after each loop that no ribbon is left beneath the binding point, see figure 68.

It is not essential that all the loops are the same size. An attractive 'waterfall' bow is made by increasing the size with each successive loop, see figure 69.

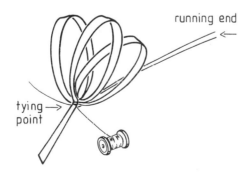

68 *Multi-loop bow*

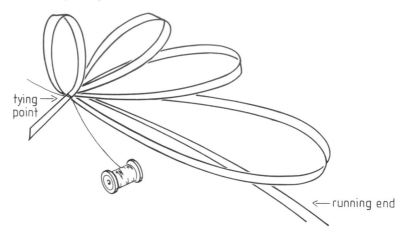

tying → point

←— running end

69 *Waterfall bow*

70 *Presentation of bouquet with bow*

Simple figure-of-eight bow This is quickly made and has a multitude of uses. The ribbon is kept flat and simply curved around exactly like the figure 8. The most understated form is two loops with a short end either side. The centre can be secured with either a matching piece of ribbon or with a taped wire. More loops may be added if a bow with more volume is required. Figures 71(a) and 71(b).

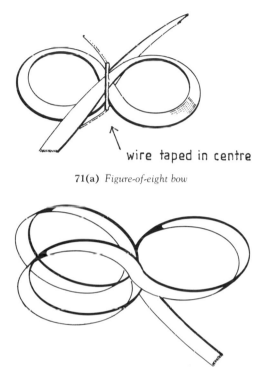

wire taped in centre

71(a) *Figure-of-eight bow*

71(b) *Securing centre of bow*

Another version of the multi-loop bow is made as follows:

1   Fold ribbon in flat loops three or four times, according to the size of bow required.

2   Carefully cut a V-shape in centre at each side. Use very sharp scissors and do not cut too deeply or the ribbon may tear.

3   Tie a narrow strip of matching ribbon across the centre. Pull each loop round and up so that they stand up; the effect is similar to that obtained with the Italian ribbon. It is not only more satisfying to construct the bow oneself, but the size of loops can also be varied to suit the occasion.

Bouquet in cellophane   Materials needed will be a roll of cellophane, a stapler, a multi-loop bow either blending or contrasting, flowers and foliage, a sachet of flower preservative and the greeting card and envelope plus a care of flowers card. Incidentally it is very attractive sometimes to incorporate two ribbons into the bow: for example, a narrow gold or silver together with the main colour, or for Christmas, try red *and* green together.

1   Have all component parts ready to hand. Select foliage carefully. Cupressus is not really suitable for a vase arrangement and should never be used unless the situation is desperate.

2   Check that all stems are clean and that there is no unsightly wood left on the foliage.

3   Arrange flowers and foliage. Try not to cut any stems; therefore keep long-stemmed material towards the top and group the shorter flowers towards the tying point. This is a very elementary point but some florists get carried away with the design and forget that the recipient may want that long stemmed flower just as it is!

4   Tie the bouquet firmly together with the decorative bow.

5   Lay the bouquet on the cellophane with sufficient overlap at the stem-end of the bouquet so that the paper can be brought over the stems right up to the tying point. This overwrap will protect the stems in transit and help to conserve the moisture within.

6   Leave enough overlap at the flower end for the cellophane to be brought right over the flowers and down to the tying point.

7   Pleat the paper in at the tying point and secure with one staple each side. Note, keep the bow and the long tie-ends *outside* the paper. If the bouquet is somewhat bulky, make a pleat in the centre of the cellophane at the tying point so that there is more volume to the overwrap.

8   Cross the long tie-ends at the back of the bouquet and bring them around to the front and tie again either through or behind the bow. Staple the cellophane together as many times as seems necessary. However, do not seal completely as otherwise the bouquet will not breathe and the paper will mist over. Figure 72.

Packing container designs
Most shops have perfected their own patent method for trans-

72 *Bouquet in cellophane*

porting designs and there are several ways of coping with the situation. The main consideration is that the arrangement shall remain steady and that the flowers are protected in all weathers.

Before packing the arrangement, pour or syphon any water out from the container, but do make sure you include a card to remind the recipient to add water on arrival. In fact, it is quite practical to carry a receptacle of water and add some to the container before handing it in. However, this is a refinement of the delivery service that not every driver would subscribe to. But do remember the card for even though the foam has already been well-soaked, it is bound to dehydrate quite rapidly in a warm atmosphere, so it is vital to the lasting quality of the design that the water level is maintained.

Special transport boxes are obtainable from most good packaging suppliers, the principal being similar to a box with a lid, in the centre of which is an adjustable aperture, see figures 73 and 74. A less costly alternative is to use a thick ceiling tile or any

73 *Packing container base for transporting*

74 *Arrangement in position*

suitable rectangle of polystyrene. The base of the container can be fixed to the tile either with *Oasis-fix* or with tape.

For a gift presentation prepare the box or tile by fixing four pieces of cellophane to the underside edges. The cellophane should be long enough to reach to the top of the design plus at least 15 cm. Fix the cellophane with *Sellotape*; do not staple as the paper may pull away. Figure 75.

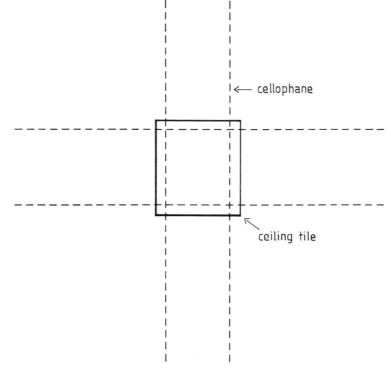

75 *Construction of container*

Having set the design in place, staple the cellophane together at the four corners, beginning at the base and securing at intervals to the top of the arrangement. Take great care not to drag the cellophane for this may damage the arrangement. Gather the paper just above the top of the design and secure it with a multiloop bow. Figure 76. Add a second bow to the other side.

A ribbon waterlily Yet another way to garnish a giftwrap, this is quickly made with a length of ribbon (the polypropylene type gives the best result) and a small stapler.

1   Make a very small loop just like the first one in a figure-of-eight bow. Secure it with one staple.
2   Make a second loop opposite the first one (again as in a figure-of-eight bow).

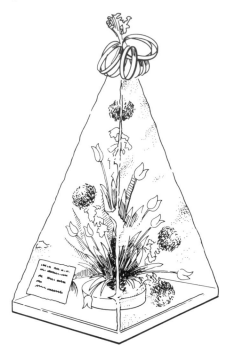

76 *Alternative type of packing container*

3   Continue making more loops, each pair slightly larger than the previous two, so that the 'waterlily' gradually increases in diameter. Secure with a staple whenever it feels necessary, but try not to use many as this will make the centre bulky.

4   Leave a long end when the flower is complete. This can be split several times and then curled with a knife blade. Tuck a short-stemmed flower into the bow; this is an extra touch that will delight the recipient.

Address labels   Position these so that the wording is easily read by the driver: near the ribbon tie on a cellophane bouquet (*not* right at the top of the presentation): near the base of an arrangement, more or less at eye level and on the end of a box of flowers. Labels should be firmly fixed with a strip.

Bouquet packaging   All packing required for transporting bridal designs, corsages, head-dresses, etc, should be prepared well before the designs are made. When they can be packed away immediately on completion, they will last far longer than if they are left on the workbench while the box is prepared. For unfortunately this does take time. There are special bouquet boxes now on the market, but they are quite expensive: some florists offer to return the cost when the box is returned to the shop, and, of course, this is a matter of policy for every individual shop to decide.

A medium-sized flower box can be covered with white paper, or with the shop's own wrapping paper. Then attach cellophane to each of the four top edges of the box. Fill the box with soft material – wood or paper shavings, polystyrene waste or even creased-up newspaper – anything that will make a soft, yet springy bed for the bouquets. Cover the lining material with white tissue paper. Make a hole through which the bouquet handle can be guided, so that the design rests safely on the soft supporting bed. Give it a last-moment spray, spread the ribbons out smoothly and fix the cellophane securely, taking care not to drag it too tightly over the design. No matter at what angle the box is held, the bouquet is secure and the bride and her family will be able to see but not handle it. If bouquets are delivered unprotected, it is a great temptation for everyone to hold them and to admire them even long before the ceremony. Complimentary to the florist though this is, it does not help the flowers to last as long as they might.

Many American florists prefer to deliver the bouquets directly to the church, which ensures not only that they are all wonderfully fresh but also that bride and bridesmaids carry them in exactly the right position.

Buttonholes, corsages and head-dresses These can sometimes be included in the bouquet box. Pin buttonholes to a ceiling tile and cover it with cellophane or a polythene bag. Corsages, also, can be secured in the same way. Be sure to fix your gold business label to the tile so that the chief wedding guests all know who has been responsible for the flowers. Head-dresses also can be fixed to a tile, depending on the shape of the design. Alternatively, make a 'head' of crushed-up tissue paper and put the designs on it.

Bascades and pomanders These should be suspended on a cane which is driven through a box, see figure 77. Pack the designs

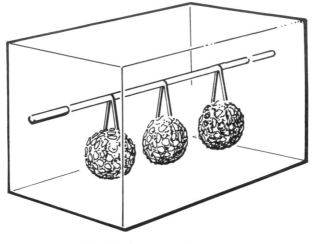

77 *Method of transporting bascades and
pomanders*

around with tissue paper so that the movement of the delivery
vehicle does not cause them to swing against the sides of the box.

Even though it is so time-consuming, good packaging should be
an integral part of your stock in trade. How far you go with gift
presentation is a matter for individual policy decisions, for one
must equate order value with time needed to complete a special
presentation. Gift packing should really be regarded as an
extension of design ability; when it is quickly and attractively
executed it expands yet another field of sales appeal.

Footnote to packaging
Think of all the items involved in this exercise – your wrapping
paper, card envelopes, business cards, letter-heading, invoices
and carrier bags (tote bags). All of these are so much part of the
everyday scene and one tends not even to see them. Your client,
however, may be seeing any or all of them for the first time. Every
one of them costs your firm quite a lot of money, so make certain
they are doing a good job for you in the field of public relations.

13 Daily work routine

To be effective, the work force in any business enterprise must realise that it is completely interdependent. Whether the team operates as two, three or twenty persons, the same basics apply. The optimum number of people involved in any particular flower shop rests, obviously, with a variety of factors, but ideally, a firm should be neither over nor understaffed. When minimum personnel becomes continuously overloaded, mistakes and frustrations will occur. On the other hand, the very nature of the flower industry dictates that there are bound to be short periods when existing staff is extremely extended, just as there are times when the pressure is off and one could logically wish for more business – all or nothing, in fact. So that to gear personnel either to peak pressure time or to 'average' or normal demand, is an exaggeration in either direction.

There the workroom manager or senior florist has to endeavour to make sure that everyone on the staff understands his or her particular facet of the work pattern so that a good grade of work can be maintained with and without supervision.

Pre-planning and delegation

The need for this cannot be overemphasised, so that even when a team is operating to the maximum there is no atmosphere of panic: rush, yes, but panic no. The day's programme, even the week's pattern, should be planned, and planned very carefully. This obviously is not just the simple process of dividing the number of items to be made by the number of staff in the workroom! For one of the particular responsibilities of senior staff is to be capable of understanding, within a little, the work-potential of the rest of the staff. Some people absolutely shine when there is almost too much to do. They genuinely enjoy working under pressure and produce their best work when operating at high speed.

On the other hand, others cannot be hurried at any price, and however high the pressure, they just cannot seem to get a move on. However, one has to be able to discern the difference between the person who CANNOT work any faster and the one who just WON'T. It has to be recognised that not every one is able to conform to a given level of output. One of the facets of good organisation is the ability to encourage the best work possible from every member of the team. It is most important that everyone on the staff feels needed, that he or she knows that the work produced, no matter what it is, plays a vital part in the work pattern of the day.

For this reason, if for no other, work should be allocated as early as possible in the day's routine. It is very discouraging, particularly for students and junior staff, to wait around for someone to find them something to do. Admittedly, there always is something to do, for sweeping, dusting and tidying are continuous activities in all flower shops. All the same, everyone ought to be given specific responsibilities as early in the day as possible for failing to do so is the quickest way to make them feel redundant. Further, it implies that the work they do is not essential which, needless to say, will speedily remove any pride of achievement.

The ideal is for the workroom manager – or whoever – to spend a few minutes the previous afternoon in discussion with all staff, deciding on plans for the following day. In so far as our last-minute type of business allows us to do this, it is an excellent idea, because it means that work can begin more quickly in the morning.

Broadly speaking the daily routine includes the following:
Despatch of prepared orders
Preparation, packing and despatch of telephone and over-the-counter orders
Stock check, for quantity and quality
Window and shop display
Conditioning of new flowers and foliage
Checking and reservation of all material needed for orders
Shop and telephone sales
Organising refreshment breaks
Routine cleaning

A formidable list, but it does not follow that the senior florist is personally responsible for doing all these operations. Quite the reverse. His or her job is to see that they are done, and in order of priority. For it is ludicrous to be concentrating on the window display when the driver is waiting to take the orders out. It is equally foolhardy to pack orders just received by telephone without first making sure that flowers that were promised for previous orders have been reserved.

Delivery lists

These should be prepared in duplicate; one copy for the driver and one as a check list for the workroom. Obviously with orders coming in all the time, it will never be quite complete, but if it has been prepared as late as possible the previous day, a fairly clear picture on several points should emerge:

1   The number and nature of timed deliveries (excluding, of course, those in the next morning's mail, over the telephone or taken in the shop)

2   Flowers required for specialist work already ordered

3   Whilst evaluating items 1 and 2, it should be possible to begin formulating a work plan for the following day.

It can be seen from this that the delivery list actually serves several very useful purposes. It not only enables your driver to see his own work pattern, and to plan accordingly. It feeds into the market list and, up to a point, helps to crystallize the day's workload.

With regard to timed funeral deliveries, it is more than likely that more will be ordered at the last moment and at times of high pressure, this is the kind of thing that threatens to make a nonsense of any well-planned delivery list. However, the average work pattern usually allows one to prepare the list of *known* orders, leaving space for additions. Cut flower and arrangement orders for no specific time will probably predominate, and the organisation must naturally be flexible enough to cope with this as it arises.

However, at no time should your driver be expected to 'beat the clock'. All orders promised for a specific time (funerals and weddings mainly) should be ready for the driver to load so that he reaches the destination safely. A clean driving licence is his work tool and he or she should never be in the position where this is put at risk.

Order checking

Despatching prepared orders This category is presumed to include funeral designs, weddings, gift arrangements and special bouquets. In fact, anything that has been prepared the previous day. Firms with cool stores have little or no problem, but even so, all work should have a last-minute check before being despatched. Shops without a cool room usually have some draught-free place to store orders, for draught, however small, is probably the worst enemy of our designs. It will soon cause de-hydration and flower-collapse. Wrapping or at least covering designs will protect them to a certain extent. Whether they are wrapped for despatch or not must be the firm's own policy decision.

Unwrapping an arrangement or a parcel of gift flowers definitely adds something to the excitement of the moment. Why, otherwise, do we bother to wrap Christmas and birthday gifts so carefully? It all contributes to the implied value of the gift. We are dealing all the time in special, personalised merchandise. It is therefore obviously in our own interests to present it looking as distinctive as possible.

Preparation and packing of current orders Cut flower orders probably predominate in this section. Some shops are spacious enough to be able to devote a special area to order packing, with all the necessary equipment handy. This is certainly the ideal arrangement. Other shops, and they are most likely in the majority, have to operate in minimal space so that most of the order packing has to be done in the shop itself. However, regardless of where the packing is done, it helps considerably if all necessary gear is to hand. Surprising how much tackle is needed to pack a bunch of flowers. A greetings card, care cards saying how to get the best from the flowers, an envelope, a packet of flower preservative, a ribbon trim, stapler, and, of course, flowers, foliage and cellophane. Also one needs to have a duster handy to keep the work surface clean.

Some shops prefer to despatch all cut flower gifts in boxes, which have a tremendous advantage over the cone wrap, as we know it in England. The contents of the box are far more protected in handling. They are more insulated against heat and cold. The orders can be piled in the delivery vehicle with the address labels fixed on the ends of the boxes.

And yet another problem arises when space is limited. Where

to put orders waiting for collection by the driver? Boxes can be safely piled on top of each other. It is probably not feasible for the senior florist to check every single order that leaves the shop. Nor should it be necessary, for if the team is operating according to plan, people should be able to work without supervision. Even so, most florists are confronted with the difficulty of selecting flowers to fill unspecified orders. For these have to include, not the flowers that the florist would like to receive, but flowers that the client thinks the recipient would like. Quite an assignment. If only customers would make their own selection instead of saying 'I leave it to you'. What makes it even more difficult is that, most likely, the florist does not know the recipient, the type of home, or colour schemes.

Yet probably at least fifty percent of cut flower orders are phrased 'a mixed bunch' thus throwing the whole responsibility of choice on the florist. Whatever the firm's policy on this situation, it must be definite that all flowers are top quality with maximum vase life, the foliage should be appropriate (fir, pine and cupressus are very suitable for funeral designs but should not be included in gift bouquets) while packing and presentation must be neat and attractive. One more point in respect of the 'mixed bunch'. How mixed is mixed? Does it mean one of this, two of that, so that the general effect resembles a fruit salad? Is the mix intended to be of types of flower, or of colour or both; after many years in the industry, these questions still remain unresolved. Possibly the most logical way to fill the orders is to ask yourself 'could I make a valid arrangement with these flowers?' If your honest answer is yes, pack the order. If there is doubt, think again. It may be that your shop has colour leaflets with sample designs, showing how to arrange gift flowers. Be sure to include one with every order for although many people really enjoy arranging their own flowers, they may still like to try something different. And this leaflet, with your firm's name and telephone, will probably be left around long after the greetings card has been thrown away. Thus, one bunch of flowers may be yet another public relations officer working for you.

As previously said, and it bears re-emphasis, packing orders takes time and concentration. Some bouquets may go to known clients, others to new ones. Either way, the packer is doing a most important part of the day's work and should, if anyhow possible, have a quiet place in which to work uninterrupted.

Reservation of material for designs

The advance orders will include funeral designs, gift arrangements and possibly some specified flowers for gift bunches, for example, roses. Reserving all these flowers should be top priority. Material for any wired funeral designs must obviously be well-conditioned, so this will be taken from existing stock. All roses for gift bunches and arrangements should be de-thorned. Try to have a special place for all reserved material and *label it all* so that none gets taken for shop sales.

Funeral designs   Before selecting flowers for tributes and other designs, first check that cards, envelopes or labels are written for each one. Try to have ribbon trims handy for it is very unprofessional to leave a design on the workbench while one goes in search of trimmings.

Flowers for sheaves and sprays should be tied in separate bunches, loosely, then labelled with price and name, and stood in water till ready to be made into the design. If all flowers are reserved in one operation, then there will be no duplication of flower content. If there are, say, more than six sheaves and sprays for one address, begin with a single-colour design and gradually mix colours and types of flowers. If you begin with a mixture, you will find difficulty in making every tribute look different. Be sure, too, that the ribbons vary. Nothing is more depressing than a row of tributes all with mauve bows, looking as though they have been produced by some impersonal machine.

Conditioning flowers and foliage, and care of plants

The trading pattern of your particular area will dictate how and when this should be done. For example, if you enjoy a busy passing trade in the early morning, then obviously you will need to have an enticing selection of merchandise on show in good time. On the other hand, if the majority of your clients emerge at mid-day, there is not so much urgency for this activity. How to condition material is dealt with in chapter 11. It is sufficient here to emphasise that someone, sometime, must be responsible for caring for new stock, for pricing it and for putting it either on display or into storage, as the situation dictates.

Shop and telephone sales

Packing and deliveries are probably going smoothly in the shop, but there is the hazard of constant interruption (for want of a better word) by the telephone and personal shoppers. Obviously these are very welcome for they all spell business, but they are yet another good reason why the senior florist or person in charge should not become too involved in any one operation, packing bouquets, for example. Someone must always be available to answer the telephone and/or to attend to shop sales. Salesman-ship is discussed in chapter 18, but it is not out of context to emphasise here that whoever answers the telephone is acting as the firm's representative. How any call is handled will reflect on the firm's public image. People usually telephone for information. Do not let anyone answer that cannot supply information. And the only difference between a telephone client and one on the shop floor is that you can see the one but not the other. Each needs help, information and possibly advice. Make sure your sales force is equipped with all necessary information, for they are people, not vending machines.

Window and shop display
Whether the window is completely redressed each day depends on the volume of work and on the staff available. It is, however, essential that it is made to look tidy as early in the day as possible. At times of peak rush, it may be necessary to clear it completely for a short time. This is certainly preferable to a display of containers almost empty of flowers and seemingly uncared-for. Some shops have moderately small window space, but are fortunate in having a considerable amount of behind-the-scenes storage space. Here the policy may be to leave the window display intact and to draw all flowers from store as needed. Some use display cool stores which are very useful indeed. The front of the cooler is all glass, usually with sliding panels, while the back of the fitment can be used for storing flowers at various levels. This kind of fitment will also serve as a divider between workroom and shop floor.

Although the routine will, perforce, be different from shop to shop, the main aim is not to permit temporary chaos to interfere with business. The early morning client has the right to be treated with just as much courtesy as the one who comes later on, when the day's work has, so to speak, smoothed out.

Put yourself in the shoes of the person obliged to call in the shop before going to work. How would you like to find yourself standing in the centre of a veritable vortex, with staff, designs, parcels and flowers literally whirling around you, and everyone too busy even to bid you good morning. An exaggeration, obviously, but that first hour or so can become chaotic if it is not very carefully planned.

And in spite of all the planning in the world, one can only take care of the known factors. The unexpected – and there is plenty of that in the flower industry – must be tackled and covered as it occurs, but not at the expense of reasonable order, serenity and sanity. This is where pre-planning will probably take care of at least sixty per cent of any problem of organisation. And by pre-planning is meant that each member of staff is doing the most important thing at the right time – Utopian, certainly, but well-worth aiming for.

Routine cleaning
After such an alarming list of demands on everyone early in the day, it is questionable whether time or energy is left to cope with anything else. On some days this may well be the case. All the same, there is a certain amount of unavoidable routine cleaning and tidying for which everyone should be made to feel responsible and at which everyone should take a turn from time to time.

Clean containers are almost as vital as clean dishes at table. It is senseless to use flower preservative if the solution is mixed in a dirty container. The easiest and quickest way to clean them is to mix a strong solution of ordinary domestic bleach in one container (take care it does not splash on your clothes). Then after about ten minutes, pour it into another container and so on. Drain each container upside-down, no need to rinse, and all should be perfectly clean. Incidentally, always drain containers upside-down so that no polluted water is left to mix with the next lot of flower water.

Constant sweeping has also been mentioned before and it is one of those ever-present jobs that all too frequently is left for 'someone else' to do. 'Someone else' is a luxury in personnel few florists can afford. Dusting and tidying, sweeping, checking equipment such as pins, order books, pens, etc, as well as washing dusters daily, are all things that, at very busy times, can so easily get pushed to one side, but someone should be made to feel responsible for them.

Lunch breaks
However busy they are, all staff should have a brief mid-morning

break and, of course, a proper lunch time. This obviously need not be organised every day, but there must be basic understanding on several points, the most important being that *not everyone downs tools at once.*

Hot drink dispensers are an effective way of coping with refreshments. On the other hand, some shops still make their own tea, coffee, etc, in which case it must be someone's responsibility to see that everything necessary is to hand. Also there should be a rota of staff who prepare the refreshment and another for the person who tidies up afterwards. This is far less wasteful in time and materials than if each does it for himself. Incidentally, do not overlook your driver who may be on the road at coffee time, so be sure he or she, also, has some refreshment, all of which must be enjoyed out of sight of the public. If the premises are large enough, there should be a rest room where staff can go one or two at a time to have their breaks. Those left know that they will have to answer the telephone or sell in the shop so that there is no question of anyone's confronting a customer while enjoying a chocolate bar or halfway through a cup of coffee, which is not only unprofessional, but bad manners.

All staff working a full day should have a proper lunch break and, as far as possible, the timing should be adhered to. One would never, for example, walk off in the middle of a sale, or indeed, halfway through a design just because the clock struck noon. But the majority of workrooms are run on a personal basis and the majority of staff is fairly flexible. Anyone obliged to leave late returns to work that much later. It is the senior florist's responsibility to see that every member of staff is taken care of in this respect, and also to make sure that no one abuses the arrangement without good reason.

It is always said that the secret of success lies in the ability to delegate. Certainly modern-day take-over agreements and giant amalgamations are not concluded while the establishment is still packing its own orders. The senior florist in the status of workroom administrator must develop the ability to recognise, analyse and then delegate. And this is a good deal more demanding than it sounds.

14 Organizing deliveries

Planning the route

Whether a shop has minimal staff or far more, very few can exist without a delivery service. True, some are now using a pool system, rather than running their own vehicles and where this works it is an excellent plan. Someone, however, has to do the deliveries, and basic planning still applies. The florist is, above all, a slave of time, but having undertaken to deliver goods in time (*note*, there is a difference between 'in time' and 'on time') they must be there. This applies particularly to designs for funerals and for bridal flowers.

The general practice is to try to deliver funeral designs just under one hour before the service, assuming, of course, that there is not too long a journey to the church. This is usually arranged with the funeral director with whom the florist should maintain a close business relationship.

Brides sometimes ask for their flowers to be brought several hours before the ceremony but – and this impinges on good salesmanship – if it is explained that possibly their home will be warm and that the designs will be far safer at the florist's shop, most of them agree to having them delivered about one hour before-hand. Certainly no bride should be made unhappy on her wedding day and in this respect, as well as for funerals, the operative phrase is 'in time'.

If the driving force is to be used to advantage, whether it be a part-time driver or a fleet of vehicles, it should not be kept waiting. This is one aspect of staff psychology that is well worth keeping in mind. This point has already been made elsewhere, but to repeat, nothing is more aggravating to a driver than to have to wait for orders and then be obliged to drive faster than is prudent to get them to their destinations on time. There are florists who have never done any delivery work themselves and one must always bear in mind that driving and delivering is a very tiring exercise. Only those who have done it regularly realise the frustration of waiting in traffic jams, of the problem of parking space and of struggling into small lifts (elevators) with large designs. And, possibly, the most frustrating of all, of trying to deliver flowers when the recipient is not at home.

Timed and untimed deliveries
Some florists find that delivery is becoming a major part of their service; for numerous reasons others are being forced to eliminate it altogether. Those who can exist without it are very fortunate: for the others, it has to be accomplished efficiently and economically, with minimum loss of time and physical effort.

A pre-planned route will help the time factor. The driver may possibly prefer to do this, as he or she will probably understand the area and the driving conditions. The delivery list will already have been prepared, though other destinations will need to be added as they occur throughout the day. Incidentally, except for early timed deliveries, it may be advisable not to get other deliveries out too soon. To the local hospitals, for example, for it is a pity to go with possibly three bouquets, only to find two or three more come in for the same destination later in the day.

The delivery list should be divided, either on one sheet or separately, according to the number of deliveries. It is essential that the driver knows what type of goods he is looking for – a funeral design, an arrangement or a gift bouquet? Try to write the name and destination as clearly as possible. Help the driver by handing out the designs to be delivered at the end of a run *first*. These will obviously be placed towards the back of the loading area. A side-loading truck is far more practical, especially with good head-room so that the driver can get right inside.

Some firms like a signature for each item delivered. Wherever possible it is certainly advisable for funerals (except tributes delivered to the home of the bereaved) and for hospitals.

The funeral design delivery list should be made out in triplicate, as one copy will help the funeral director. That leaves one as a check list for the workroom and one for the driver. This is assuming that the tributes are, in the main, delivered to the funeral director. If they are taken to the home of the bereaved, they, also, may appreciate a copy.

Specimen delivery list for funeral designs

Tributes for the funeral of the late ....
on date.......... at time.......... c/o name of funeral director.

Item	Card inscription
Yellow cross	Love from Bill
Wreath	George and Alice
Basket	Amanda and Jane

Received in good condition   Time . . .

Signature . . . .   Date . . .

Specimen delivery sheet for miscellaneous designs

Type of design	Address	No.	To pay	Signature
Arrange— ments		2	–	None
"		1	£10	
"		5	–	
Bouquets	Hospital	4	–	
"	Old people's home	3	–	
"		1	–	None
Plants				
"		3	–	

The invoice for the arrangement should either be clipped to the delivery sheet or attached to the design *in an envelope.*

Non-delivery

This concerns addresses at which there is no reply and sometimes happens when an unexpected gift is being delivered. Sometimes a friendly neighbour will agree to take care of the gift (always get a signature) but if not, the only alternative is to bring the article back to the shop, unless you know the recipient very well and know the gift can safely be left in a garage or other suitable place.

Make sure that there are always some cards in the vehicle stating that delivery has been attempted, asking that the recipient will telephone to make arrangements for a second delivery. Sometimes he or she will volunteer to collect the gift; otherwise it is possible to agree a day when someone will be at home. Either way it minimises pressure on the driving force; it also diminishes the risk of wasting flowers, for obviously, if the person is going to be away for several days, the florist can at least absorb the flowers back into stock.

These non-delivery cards should be designed so that there is no doubt that this is a business communication and not a circular. They should be about postcard size, certainly no smaller, possibly bright yellow or shocking pink, with bold lettering on one side saying 'Your Florist Has Called'. The reverse should contain all the necessary information so that contact can be made with the shop as soon as possible.

```
When we called to deliver flowers to you
today, we could not obtain an answer
    ┌───┐  The flowers have been returned to
    │ ✓ │
    └───┘  the shop: please telephone us.
    ┌───┐  The flowers have been left with
    │   │
    └───┘
    _____

Name, address and telephone number of shop
```

The following few points may be obvious, but are worth mentioning. Try always to get maximum information about an address. The name of a house is not enough; in some districts they are not visible from the road. In rural areas, ask for a landmark. If the recipient happens to be a visitor to the house, and this does occur, ask the name of the householder. Local people often know their neighbours' names but cannot know the names of all their visitors. Get a telephone number as well, if possible, for if a real problem arises, then you can telephone for instructions. It is, of course, a pity to have to do so, for it removes the element of surprise, but this is better than non-delivery.

Vehicle responsibility

Damage If by some mischance a bouquet or arrangement should get damaged in transit, ask the driver always to bring it back. Never knowingly deliver a damaged article. A multitude of circumstances could give rise to this situation – possibly faulty packing; slightly careless or hasty handling or, the most likely of all, a sudden emergency stop.

Equip your driver with small change, enough to make a

telephone call back to base. For a conscientious driver will always call in for information rather than driving all the way back to the shop. However, try to resolve all queries before departure, because probably you will not only be delaying one particular parcel, but a complete delivery run.

Most drivers do this type of work because they enjoy it. They like getting out and about rather than being tied to a desk or workbench. However, they are not magicians, nor paragons of patience, so do not expect the impossible. It must be someone's specific responsibility to check items out of the shop with the driver, and to see that each time he or she returns, time is not wasted in standing around. Neither does it follow that he must be hustled from one journey to another reminiscent of an old Laurel and Hardy film. He is a vital member of the team and it is worth spending a few moments discussing the day's programme, so that he, too, can identify with the pattern of events. If it looks like being a fairly quiet day, then take advantage of it; maybe clean the vehicle, have it serviced or take care of other necessary odd jobs that have to be shelved when everyone is on full pressure.

It may seem strange that a whole chapter is devoted to the machinery of delivery. But generally speaking, if the competitive and ambitious florist is to give the type of service expected by the public this facet of business is very important. It calls for a delivery force that is not only top rate in getting around the area and delivering the goods, but who, it must be recognised, is acting as your front person, who carries your public image right into the home, or hospital or wherever. For it could be that your driver is the only member of your team ever seen by some customers. For example, the lucky recipient of a gift of flowers may never have been into your shop, and will judge it in the first moment, by the appearance and demeanour of your driver. In our busy south-London shop we had one driver who was so liked by the customers that one, a handicapped lady, persuaded him to walk her dog whenever he delivered a bouquet. In fact, he built up a small but appreciative 'inner clientele' of customers who needed small services and from time to time, brought more flower orders back to the shop. He also brought back snippets of information that helped the florists to identify with homes and people that were simply names and addresses to them. So make sure that he or she feels part of the team.

On the other side of the coin, the driver should understand that while he is driving the firm's vehicle, it is his responsibility in every respect. It is his business to ensure that it is in good running order, kept topped up with fuel and oil and that the spare tyre is ready to use if the need arises. He should immediately report any fault so that it can be put right at the earliest possible moment. Make all this abundantly clear at the time of hiring. Whether or not you expect him to be responsible for cleaning must rest with the firm's policy, but the interior should be kept clean so that each package comes out as fresh as when it left the workroom. The driver and vehicle is the firm's mobile publicity force. If the vehicle is clean and neat with the firm's sign and name and address on it, the driver will be proud to be seen in charge of it. Your clients will be proud to have it drive up to the residence, so that it is clear that they deal only with the best people. There is absolutely no doubt that a smart delivery vehicle can do a great deal to enhance your public image.

Vehicle service   Finally, if you know nothing at all about motor mechanics keep in mind that all vehicles need regular servicing. This is all the 'mechanics' you need to know. Let a reliable garage take care of it at whatever the specific mileage is for regular service. Your driver can keep the mileage check and remind you to make an appointment with the garage. This is so much easier than waiting for everything to stop and then having to get it put right.

15 Customer relations

Customer relations should not be confused with salesmanship, though the two do, in fact, overlap in certain aspects. The dictionary defines the word 'customer' as 'a person who buys, especially one who buys regularly'.

This is most encouraging, for it leads one to presuppose that the person who buys automatically becomes the customer who buys regularly. And surely this is exactly what we are all trying to establish. The chance customer of today becomes *our* customer of tomorrow, of next week and, we hope, regularly throughout many years.

Numerous factors contribute to a happy business relationship. What inspires people to buy what they do where they do? This is a truly fascinating and compelling question for anyone engaged in retail business. Such a compelling subject, in fact, that specialist organisations devote all their time and energy into research on the subject.

To have a successful business relationship, is it enough to sell high-quality merchandise? Is it sufficient to have a clean, tidy shop and a civil staff? Although these are high ideals to aim for in retail business, neither the one nor the other, or a combination of both, will ensure good business.

For in spite of automation, of self-service, of all the factors intended to make our daily life more efficient and flow more easily, not forgetting the all-powerful ever-present faceless computer, successful business relationships ultimately boil down to the human element. For the florist is dealing not only in perishable merchandise; he handles delicate human relationships. The anxious new father, buying red roses for his wife after the birth of their firstborn, appreciates interest in what – to him – is an exciting and novel experience. Naturally, the florist is primarily concerned with selling red roses, but it costs nothing to show interest, to wish the family happiness and to enquire about the new baby's name. This is not idle curiosity; it is a means of establishing customer relations, by indicating that you care about this particular situation.

It is possible that the very next customer will be ordering flowers for a funeral. Sympathy and understanding of the highest degree is needed in this situation. It calls for a delicate balance of human relationship for the florist to offer considered advice yet also to conclude what, after all, must be a satisfactory business deal.

One could continue a catalogue of various circumstances involving the sales force. For example, flowers to a hospital patient; a bouquet to say thank you for an enjoyable weekend; bon voyage flowers to a traveller and one that will always be recalled with what could be termed benevolent curiosity. A flower relay order for a bouquet costing a generous amount of money with the one word 'sorry'. 'Goodness knows what he's done,' said the florist on the sending end of the order, 'but let's hope this puts things right'.

Every transaction involves human relationships and the florist would be very hard-boiled not to be even vaguely interested in each situation; not only hard-boiled but very short-sighted. For people might buy once in a store that has a cold, impersonal atmosphere, but they would not readily return to such an unfriendly situation.

Customer relations is a nebulous business asset that should be constantly worked on. Of course, top-grade merchandise is of prime importance and it is just as vital that the sales force understands all facets of the business, otherwise they will not be in a position to give advice and help. Even the layout of the shop will make a difference to the prevailing atmosphere. Is there an air of welcome when the customer first steps inside? The chances are that if the shop is well-planned from the staff point of view, then it will also be agreeable from the other side of the counter. Though this phrase, today, is somewhat outdated for so many shops, particularly flower shops, have adopted the open-plan design which, happily, does away with the feeling of segregation enforced by an imposing counter.

During the last few years, there has been immense advance in the science of shop fitting and lay-out. Much of this is, unfortunately, costly, but changes and improvements can, indeed should be made gradually. For in a flower shop, very few fittings should be absolutely static, because it is constantly necessary to vary the display. It is far easier to do this if most of the fittings are moveable.

Floor coverings, lighting and display accessories all help to set the scene. It is a good idea to get expert advice on both flooring and/or covering and lighting since unsuitable materials can cost just as much as the right thing. Correct lighting is very important, not only for displaying the merchandise, but also for speed and ease of working.

But what has all this to do with customer relations? A fair question, but in point of fact, it is all contributory to the general atmosphere within the shop, which in turn has direct bearing on good business – or not, as the case may be.

Dealing with complaints   From time to time, you are bound to encounter the difficult, or even the disgruntled client. It would be idle to pretend that one's business day could progress gently along without problems of one sort or another. From the client's point of view, if he or she needs to lodge a complaint, one of the most tactful ways of doing this is to use the telephone. I once used this approach having asked to speak to the person in charge: 'I am obliged to make some comments which I believe you would prefer your other customers not to hear'. We were then able to discuss the problem and the matter was concluded reasonably amicably.

However, if your customer really wants to be difficult, then he or she states the case forcibly and loudly in the middle of the shop for all to hear. Such a situation can and, unfortunately, does occur and it takes a good deal of experience to cope with it satisfactorily.

The first rule to apply when confronted with this type of situation, is to listen. Generally speaking, human nature is relatively extrovert and once someone has been able to state his case, to let off steam, so to speak, he immediately begins to feel better. And, of course, from the purely business point of view, how can one possibly evaluate any situation without first knowing the facts? The question will be, what exactly are the facts. This you will never know unless you are prepared to listen. But the sales floor is certainly not the ideal arena for the exercise. So, once the customer pauses for breath, invite him into your office, or gently edge him towards it if unable to get a word in edgeways!

It is amazing what a chair and a cup of coffee and/or a cigarette will do to help iron out a situation that threatens to get tangled up in too much rhetoric. As the manager or principal, one is naturally tempted to justify oneself, or the firm, or the staff, or all three perhaps, a moment or so too soon.

One is not obliged to take up an attitude at this stage. It may be that the customer's complaint really is justified. It may be that it is totally unjustified, or the truth may lie somewhere between these two poles. But the case must be stated and you must evaluate the circumstances so that you can formulate your policy. Always remember that you are dealing with a human being, albeit a very irate one, and not a reject on a production line. By the same token, your customer should get the identical impression – and this is your trump card. Let it show that you realise that he or she, also, is a person, thus demonstrating beyond all doubt that you are a sympathetic being and not just a conveyor belt for perishable merchandise. The way to do this is to listen and to show both interest and concern.

It is nothing like so easy to be interested in the disgruntled client as in the customer who is actually buying something, but the cold fact remains that your best equipment for this unfortunate area of customer relations is patience, sympathy and understanding, as well as a good deal of honesty with yourself. If something has gone wrong with your client's order – or he has the idea that it has – find out exactly what and why. Again it boils down to the human element. There is probably a logical reason somewhere along the line. When you find it, let your client know, either with a personal visit to his home, or by letter or over the telephone. Never invite him to call into the shop; it could start the dialogue up all over again and you would find yourself going round in ever-decreasing circles.

One final point: if you feel that, for some reason or other, your stock of patience, interest and understanding is at a low ebb, then ask someone else to handle the situation. If there is no one else, write the details down and tell your client that you will look into the matter. The chances are that you will have to anyway, but the main thing is that he must be assured that something is being done.

There may well be other members of staff who can assume this responsibility. Make sure you use them. Be honest enough to recognise that they may have more patience than you have. It could be that you are temporarily short of sleep, you have some personal anxiety or that your patience has already been extended beyond the reasonable. Then accept the situation. This is not shirking your responsibilities. It is being mature enough to put your customer first.

16 Staff relations

Large organisations employ a personnel officer whose sole function is to take care of everything relating to the well-being of the staff, and to deal with any questions that arise between management and personnel. For it is widely recognised that no business can operate to maximum efficiency if staff are working in an atmosphere of tension or resentment. This type of atmosphere can be engendered by any number of influences, but it is the senior florist's responsibility to try to ensure that everything runs smoothly. This does not mean, however, that he or she should, every waking moment, be listening to small grumbles that might arise from, possibly, a clash of personalities. But all staff should feel that there is someone in authority who can be approached without actually going to the boss.

This is not one of the most agreeable facets of senior staff responsibility for it can prove very difficult to arbitrate between other members of staff who are, presumably, not only your colleagues, but your friends. Two main points, however, must be recognised. One is that sometimes a given situation is not necessarily anyone's 'fault'. People with a grievance tend to say something like 'if he or she had not done this or said that, I would not be obliged to take up this attitude'. It may be so and they may well be right. On the other hand, such dialogue rarely leads to a solution of the situation. For, if an acrimonious situation persists, one has to look for the cause, which could be something quite simple, such as a small adjustment in the workroom plan. On the other hand, it might be a factor that is not so easily resolved: a matter of personal chemistry. In other words, two people, each admirable in his or her own way, yet causing a clash of will-power if expected to work together.

Senior staff should be sophisticated enough to recognise when a situation has to be referred to a higher level, or whether the circumstances can be ironed out to everyone's satisfaction (well, more or less) through discussion between the parties concerned.

In endeavouring to assess any situation it should be remembered that a good florist is part technician and part artist. Therefore allowance has to be made for artistic temperament if a reasonably tranquil working atmosphere is to be maintained. This seems rather bad luck on the senior florist or workroom manager, for who makes allowances for temperament here? It is to be hoped that tact and diplomacy will not be overtaxed too often, and if it is, then there is something radically wrong and it is time for serious discussion. For on no account must a situation be allowed to stay 'on the boil' so that feelings run high and logical judgment becomes warped.

Everyone has a different level of toleration. Some will put up with things that others could not possibly stand for one moment. This is all part of the mystery of personality. It must be one of the prime loyalties of the job of senior staff to try to understand the team; to realise that when one person has a little grumble, it is just letting off steam, yet when another one does precisely the same thing, it should be taken seriously. The first character has a low level of tolerance, yet in spite of small explosions from time to time, is probably an easier mentality to comprehend. The second one is given to bottling things up, so that when finally something is said, it is as well to take the situation seriously. There are many levels of tolerance, there are many facets to people's characters, but possibly the biggest menace to a contented team is the sulk. This is the personality who has, or who appears to have, a grievance, but who will not or cannot put it into words; who creates an untenable atmosphere but who will rarely state the problem. Fortunately they are rare but should be dealt with firmly and fairly. After all, no one is forced to work for a particular firm and if he or she does not like the situation, then the simplest thing is to find another place to work.

Basics of good staff relations

General wellbeing of everyone is a good premise on which to build; the more tangible aspects of workroom administration, which should include:

* sufficient working space for each member of staff
* good light
* sufficient heat and ventilation

* proper storage space for equipment
* good washroom facilities with running hot water
* hanging space for outdoor clothes
* seats for every staff member
* a private area or staffroom where everyone can take a lunch break and make a hot drink

Vending machines are very convenient for quick refreshment as well as doing away with all the tackle required to make cups of tea or coffee, and there is no washing up afterwards!

Since all members of the team are expected to maintain a neat and attractive appearance, it is vital that there is an adequate powder room with mirror and running hot water. Agreed that flower shop premises are frequently very limited, but even so, there are certain basics that should be provided without question. Dirty hands and stained finger nails need not be an occupational hazard, but neither should florists be expected to wash in cold water.

Private telephone calls Several decades ago it was an unwritten, yet firmly enforced law that no one in commerce had private telephone calls during working hours, either in or out. Fortunately this viewpoint has relaxed and a much happier atmosphere of give and take prevails in most firms. This may seem a minor point, but it is something that could build up to a major incident if tolerance and understanding is not exercised on both sides. Prolonged calls consume valuable time and also tie up a business line. But on the other hand, it is no longer logical to expect staff to bisect their lives neatly down the middle, with private life on one side and shop life on the other.

Time off There are times when someone may need a day or part of a day off, for any number of reasons, from visits to the dentist to the proverbial much-abused one of a grandparent's funeral. All members of the team, from the youngest to the most senior, should feel that they can ask for time away from work, provided the reason is fairly explained, without being penalised. From the management angle, if time off is not granted, then staff will take 'sick leave' and thereafter mutual trust vanishes.

Annual holidays Staff vacation should be arranged as early as possible in the year so that everyone knows the pattern. Those with children in school or very young members of the team, who have to take their holidays with parents, will most likely have to receive first consideration. It is vital that all members of staff have adequate holidays and they should be encouraged to take two weeks at once rather than two separate weeks. No one can work at the pace of a busy flower shop without a proper break away from routine. A third week, or long weekend, taken either late in the year or just after Christmas quite remarkably contributes towards minimising sickness and consequently, absenteeism.

Similarly, the boss should also be able to take a vacation. If he is usually very active in the business his absence will obviously put a weight of responsibility on the staff; in fact, every single member of the team should be missed when not there. However, a tired niggly boss is not the happiest of working companions and it is in everyone's interest that he has a fair break along with everyone else. Obviously, everyone must assume a little more responsibility, but it should be possible to ensure that the business keeps rolling just for a week or so.

Staff shopping   When several members of the firm have access to the cash point, it is in everyone's interest to have a firm policy which is not relaxed in any circumstances. Naturally it should be possible for personnel to buy articles from the firm; any discount arrangements are also matters of individual policy. But rather than just putting the cash in the drawer, the drill should be on the lines of the purchasing member of staff handing the money to another colleague, who treats the transaction in the same manner as if it had been a client.

People not closely connected with retail business sometimes have the notion that all the money in the cash register simply has to be scooped into the boss's pocket when the store closes and that is that. But a cash register is really just a handy receptacle for the day's takings which, as every business man knows, will be fiercely decimated when the firm's commitments need to be met: not the least of these being the staff salaries. It cannot be emphasised too strongly that the cash register should be regarded as everyone's responsibility.

These precautions add up to mutual trust all round, and not the reverse, as might be imagined.

Fidelity   The administration (probably quite simply 'the boss') also has certain points of view that should be respected. For instance, when personnel is hired, they enter into a contract with the organisation. The work is explained and the rate for the job is stated. The hired hand, by accepting the situation, agrees to the conditions and hours of work and, of course the pay. Everyone should adhere to this agreement.

Staff should make every effort to get to work on time. Some people are naturally punctual, others genuinely find it difficult ever to be on time for anything. But members of a team who make a habit of beginning work late are not only short-timing the boss, they are short-timing their colleagues, because it means that someone else has to fill in for them meanwhile. When anyone arrives late, it is reasonable to expect an explanation. Similarly if the boss is detained, he or she should have the basic civility to let the staff know. For if a loyal, energetic and responsible team is to be built up, civility and loyalty must be a two-way process.

On the subject of loyalty, personnel at all levels must clearly understand that their work is confidential. Orders placed by clients should never be discussed outside the premises, not even with close members of the family. The contents of card messages and the value of orders is also confidential between client and firm. In some instances a great deal of trust is placed in the firm and it must never be betrayed.

The staff team   Although major policy-making and the taking of top level decisons rests with the administration, it is obvious that effective staff must work as a team. The dictionary defines the word team: 'to join in co-operative activity'. This completely sums up the day-to-day effort of the staff of a busy flower shop. A team does not just happen, it has to be built up gradually, through mutual trust and understanding amongst its members. Like a good orchestra, it needs constant practice to present a finished performance to the public. This is exactly what the florist aims to do – to present a smooth and sophisticated performance to the client, both in actual work and in shop atmosphere.

The effective team will only operate to maximum efficiency when every member knows his or her particular area of responsibility, when everyone understands the general picture and when all are aiming at the same goal. Yet each member of the team should be flexible enough in outlook and ability to be able to switch duties and to assume, from time to time, unexpected responsibilities. The senior florist should be able to evaluate when a student is ready for more responsibility, but should never overload him so that he becomes despondent. It must be recognised that people have different speeds of comprehension and just because someone seems slow doing one operation it does not follow that he is without capabilities in another direction. And the converse also applies. The person who adapts to manual techniques rapidly does not necessarily become the best managerial material. So the senior florist or manager should use each member of the team according to their particular capabilities; this results in a far better feed-back than taking the attitude 'this needs to be done and it's your turn to do it'.

However, there are bound to be days when the staff ask themselves why on earth they ever signed up with such a mean boss. There must also be moments when the boss wonders how he ever came to be stuck with such a ham-handed ineffective team. This is inevitable, particularly where the personal element and a certain amount of temperament is involved on both sides. But tolerance, understanding, civility and a sense of humour – that above all – ought to be capable of finding a way of bridging any small gaps that threaten the fabric of the team as a whole.

17 Peak period organisation

The simple solution to any pressure of work, in whatever field, is to understand the situation and to organise against all known eventualities. How easy that sounds in cold print, in fact rather smug. For there can be few of us whose lives have not been beset at some time with undue pressure. Working against a deadline in the office and handicapped by a raging headache; trying to organise house and garden, plus domestic animals so that one can take a much-needed vacation, or the ever-present daily pressure of running a household in which everyone's needs vary and the whole family expects everything to be done yesterday!

The one difference in these examples as compared with the flower shop – or any shop, for that matter – is that one is not exposed to the public. Not that the florist wants to abolish peak time business for a whole year of even trade, neither too slow nor too fast, would be totally colourless and utterly without challenge.

There are several factors involved in getting on top of these peak time rushes:

1 To recognise where the pressure is most acute – with the sales force; the driving team; office and telephone; stock checking and ordering; packing deliveries. These are all very sensitive areas that should be carefully evaluated.
2 Understanding the above pre-supposes that the principal, whether he or she is the shop-owner or high-level managerial staff, thoroughly understands the job, which obviously involves long years of training and experience.

Record keeping
For the flower industry in Britain, the most stressful times are, naturally, Christmas and Mothers' Day, St Valentine's Day and,

in some areas, Jewish New Year. However, these are not sudden happenings; from year to year we all have reasonable hope that they will come round again in another twelve months. This means then, that in theory there are about eleven months to plan and prepare. Of couse it never works out quite like that, but what it does mean is that as soon after the peak season as possible, the florist should make a plus and minus list. Plus for the things that went well (repeat again next year only more so); minus for the converse (this needs looking into and how can we make it go more smoothly in the future?).

Accepting that no shop can function without enough stock of the right kind at all times, this is top priority. Records should be kept of what is bought – when and where and in what volume, also what was paid for it.

This sounds a terrible chore. So it is for the first year, but the time and pressure saved in subsequent years will make the exercise thoroughly worthwhile. Incidentally, these records should not just be a clip containing all your receipts, but everything should be kept in diary form so that the necessary information can be referred to quickly.

It is, of course, to be hoped that business is on the increase all the time, so your ordering this year should be well in advance of the quantities logged for last year. The suppliers of all perishable merchandise will also appreciate an advance order signal.

Advance ordering not only applies to perishable stock, but to all regular background items as well. Wrapping paper, ribbons, greetings cards, envelopes, foam, containers, order pads, pens, dusters, staplers; the list seems almost endless. Keeping the level of all non-perishable stock up seems easy; one just orders and puts it on the shelf and if you have over-ordered, the item will get used in time, not depreciate like your perishables. But there is a snag: the simple question of storage space. So only buy ahead as much as can be properly stored, but do be sure to have a final check at least six weeks before peak time to ensure delivery well before the pressure begins to build up.

Publicity

There is a school of thought which maintains that it is unnecessary to plug merchandise for peak times when people are buying anyway. Like all debate, there are two points of argument. Certainly more people are buying more merchandise, but are they buying from your shop? And this, obviously, is what you want to motivate. For example, are you offering anything different from last year? Has your delivery area expanded? Do you carry new, exciting ranges in dry goods, in containers, ribbons, accessories? What will be the cut-off date for accepting orders for arrangements? You must do everything in your power to inform and persuade, not only your own clientele but that vast untapped area of potential customers (yes, they do exist!) that your merchandise and your special brand of service is exactly what they were looking for, to help solve their gift problems.

To help reduce last-minute pressure, some stores offer discount on anything ordered, paid for and carried away no less than one week beforehand. This certainly takes some of the pressure off the deliveries.

There are some aspects of peak-time organisation that apply at every festival: stock levels, staff and extra help, delivery planning, etc. But while it is generally a slow build-up towards the last few days before Christmas Eve, thus spreading the load somewhat, Mothers' Day and St Valentine's Day are – to quote a colleague – Christmas week condensed into one day.

Key points
Extra help in the sales area With certain reservations people from any age group would be helpful here. Obviously the basic requirement is that they must enjoy selling; up to a point they should understand the stock; they should move quickly and economically and be endowed with abundant commonsense (for this often prevails when technical know-how is absent). It seems a tall order, but in fact, there are people possibly in the upper age groups, who have already had sales experience in other fields, and who would prove to be invaluable. It sometimes happens, even, that permanent help is recruited from this part-time help.

But do not expect everyone to arrive already equipped with these abilities; packing flowers and plants is a specialist skill. Staff, part-time help, that is, should be shown how to do it. They should never be left marooned to muddle through as best they can. Thus, all temporary help must be recruited early enough for them to be briefed well before the major rush. Then there is also time to do any necessary 'weeding out' of anyone who fails to fit into the team.

Unless the same people are hired year after year (and this is, of course, the ideal situation) temporary help should not be expected to come equipped with tools, other than a pen. Scissors, a knife, an overall, should be supplied by the management, so that for the time they are with the firm, they both look and feel as if they belong.

Extra help in the workroom   This entails making ribbon bows which are stockpiled in large clear polythene bags, general checking of supplies such as wires, ribbons, etc, emptying containers, replenishing perishable stock and, possibly, conditioning new stock.

Telephone   If the shop does not have a full-time secretary, this is a very sensitive area, for orders will be coming in from colleagues (the relay services); from known customers and from new ones. The telephone in a flower shop is always a vital tool; at peak times it is more so. Therefore whoever is in charge, should be in possession of all the facts: how to take a flower relay order; how to send one, including using the directories correctly. Telephone staff must know the current prices of all merchandise; they should, if possible, have some office experience; they need patience, a sense of humour and should, this above all, answer the telephone efficiently and with a smile, for there is no doubt that a smile, or not, is heard in the voice.

It speeds up the order-packing process tremendously if all orders are 'processed' at the time of taking, whether it be in the shop or over the telephone. This is say, write the card, the address envelope, add any care cards relevant and clip all to the order. Do not staple as this sometimes defaces the message card.

It is vital that mistakes do not occur at these times of pressure; that is, an error in date or content of an order; was it paid for in advance, or not? If your booking system is working well and can be understood by everyone taking orders, you have no problem. Here is a very simple system that is easily understood, that leaves minimal margin for mistakes.

Cash sales   These are the simplest transactions of all, since the merchandise is selected, paid for and carried away. No record is required, except to ensure that the customer has some type of identification with your shop, possibly a business card or brochure to carry away, for future orders.

Advance orders These must be taken in duplicate, with every detail itemised. It may be that the customer writes the card. The sales staff should write the address envelope, add the care cards, if any and attach to the *top copy* of the order for filing on the appropriate day in the workroom. If it is paid for at the time, then the customer carries away the receipt.

If it is not paid for – and this, obviously, applies to all telephoned orders – the second copy is your record for the accounts department. This sounds very high level, but one of the safest and most foolproof accessories is an old-fashioned spike on to which one can impale the accounts copy. These can later be checked by whoever is in charge of accounts, entered, and invoices typed and despatched.

Customer movement Before the rush begins, check around the sales area to see if any fitments could be re-sited to allow for more movement space. It may be logical to remove some fitments altogether just for the time being. You will want to have as much display space as possible, but remember there will be more customers than usual in the shop and they will need space to move around. Double check the position of the wrapping bench; might it speed things up to have a second one just for the duration? Check, also, the siting of the cash register, for a bottle-neck can build up around this area.

Take a similar look at the workroom lay-out; consult the staff and get their views on how things are working and apply some elementary time and motion study to the situation. As an experiment I once wore a pedometer through the Christmas season. In one day it registered ten miles, simply walking between workroom and sales floor – no wonder florists are tired by Christmas Eve!

Cash point The cash register should be sited so that the drawer opens towards the sales staff and away from the public. However, the figures recorded should always be clearly visible to the customer. Clarify with all part-time sales help whether they are expected to handle cash. If so, make sure that your type of cash register is fully understood, as well as the particular discipline involved in handling other people's money, that is, the firm's and the customer's.

Senior permanent staff should ensure that there is always

sufficient change available. Keep an extra supply so that it can be topped up when necessary, for no one should ever leave the cash drawer open while having to search for more small change. Bank notes should be placed in a separate clip or held in one hand while change is counted out. This will ensure there is no question as to the value of the note tendered. Change should be counted to the customer for this adds up to common politeness, rather than just giving a bunch of coins back without comment. At the risk of trespassing on the area of salesmanship techniques, remember that receiving the change will be the customer's final impression of the sales transaction. Giving change and handing over the merchandise with a smile will forge a personality bond between the sales staff and the client. And to add 'thank you – have a nice day' costs nothing.

Packing flower orders   The ideal situation is for some members of staff to be responsible for packing, uninterrupted by telephone or sales floor activities. For packing hundreds of orders develops into a production-line exercise and complete concentration is required if mistakes are not to be made. The orders will already have been sorted into delivery routes (or, at least, the general area, for the driver may prefer to plot the actual route). They can then be divided into order value so that those for the same value can be filled with identical flowers. It must be decided in advance what shall be used to fill which orders and these flowers put aside, together with enough foliage already cut into suitable lengths. This is another way in which temporary workroom staff can help. Orders that specify inclusion of any particular flowers should be packed, or at least reserved, to make sure that those special flowers are not, in the meantime, sold in the shop.

Extra help for deliveries   Make sure all part-time drivers have a valid licence and insurance. For obvious reasons they should know the district really well. Taxi-drivers, some students, housewives, active retired people, any or all of these may prove really useful. For one point is very certain: however well you, as manager or senior staff know your area, you should definitely not be doing the deliveries at these times of peak rush. Even though normally you take care of deliveries yourself, your expertise and experience is far more valuable at these times in the shop.

It speeds up the delivery runs if each driver can have a helper on board; someone who can quickly identify house numbers and road names (for in most parts of Britain both these are notoriously difficult to locate). Try to get the majority of the orders despatched in daylight: even so, each driver should be equipped with a reliable flashlight.

Most, if not all the foregoing applies to all times of extra pressure. But both Mothers' Day (or Mothering Sunday as it is more generally known in Britain) and St Valentine's Day present special problems, particularly those of packing and deliveries. For whereas orders may be despatched several days before Christmas, those for St Valentine's Day and Mothering Sunday have to be condensed into one day. Neither can your advance orders for these two festivals give much guide as to the final day's business for on both occasions, with perhaps a slight bias towards St Valentine's Day, there is a good deal of impulse buying. Therefore your order for red roses which, at the time of placing it, seemed unreasonably profligate, may prove only just enough at the end of the day. For to be sold out of red roses by mid-day may be satisfying for the florist in one sense, but you, by the same token, will be obliged to disappoint a number of last-minute impulse buyers. And on that point, try to despatch as many orders early in the day as possible, for these may well generate more orders.

Both Mothers' Day and St Valentine's Day are great opportunities for shop sales, so have bouquets in cellophane all ready, in varying price ranges. Customers like to see immediately what they can expect for a certain sum; you will find you sell these 'cash and carry' bouquets faster than you can make them.

Self-preservation
Having tried, in theory at any rate, to cover most eventualities that might beset the unwary, we must also do everything possible to ensure the health and comfort of the staff, in fact, the whole team, which naturally, includes the management.

1   Before a build-up of high-pressure business, try to get some extra sleep. Suggest to all staff that they do the same.

2   If overtime has to be worked, make sure it is kept within reason. It has been proved that time spent in organising will considerably reduce overtime. Those that work late should not begin so early the following morning, whilst staff that arrives early

should be the first to leave. Wherever possible, get staff taken home door to door, so that they do not have to wait about for public transport.

3   Take reasonable breaks for refreshment. There is no virtue in working yourself to a standstill, or in being a martyr and trying to exist on a succession of cups of tea. Ensure that everyone, at all levels, has adequate breaks. Even ten minutes spent in cutting out from the pressures, and in having a quiet snack, will give most people fresh motivation.

4   Do not forget to thank the team for their hard work. True, the wage packet will say most of it, but everyone works better when they know they are appreciated, and a sincere 'thank you for helping' goes a long way to building a real team.

All this, then, is the theory of the exercise. But how will it work out in actual practice? There are bound to be moments of aggravation, of frustration, of near-panic. Whatever happens, such alarms and excursions must be for off-stage only. For the client is still the most important person in your shop, both to him or herself and to you. However, if a difficulty arises that affects his particular order, then he is entitled to a clear explanation of the circumstances. He will more than likely prove to be both understanding and tolerant, for remember, some clients have businesses of their own and appreciate the difficulties and pressures.

As senior management, it is your main job to keep cheerful, calm and positive – you will be both surprised and gratified how much of this rubs off on the team.

18 Salesmanship

The essence of a good sale is balance. Balance is necessary between you, as the vendor, and your customer as the purchaser. At the conclusion of a sale there should be mutual satisfaction that the balance has, in fact, been achieved.

The seller must:
> gain the confidence of the customer
> assess correctly his or her requirements and spending capacity
> guide the customer towards a fair and satisfactory purchase
> conclude a sale that is economically satisfactory to both employer and to the flower industry
> implant the firm's image in the mind of the customer.

The customer should:
> receive courtesy and understanding
> have hesitation and uncertainty guided to a clear intention to purchase
> have complete confidence in your personality as the representative of the industry and of your employer
> complete a purchase that is within his spending power that is both fair and satisfactory
> subconsciously register an intention to shop with you again.

Study the preceding analysis of the balance of selling carefully. From the very beginning you, the salesperson, have the advantage in the fact that the potential customer is in the shop. True, this may be no more than an initial hesitant enquiry, but if you care about selling, your position is really strong. For you have around you all the eloquence of good display, and the visual persuasion that only the flowers themselves can give. But never lean on this too hard; it is you and you alone who have to negotiate the business side of the sale and its balance, or not, depends upon your competence as a salesperson.

Initially the mood of the customer may range from hesitation to the clear intention of making a predetermined purchase. But of two facts you can be quite certain: the customer is there, in the shop, voluntarily, to consult you about flowers: secondly, some expenditure is envisaged.

The choice

Always remember that the flowers, whether a simple bunch, an arrangement, a gift in cellophane, are destined to fulfil the customer's inclinations and sentiments. Thus, the eventual choice must be his – or at least, he must be led to think this is so. For your role is to advise, to guide, not just to stand there, pencil poised, waiting for the cold details of 'what and how much'. The 'what' is, of course, vital to the transaction. The 'how much' should wait a moment or so until a firm basis of mutual understanding has been established.

The type of dialogue destined to kill a balanced sale stone-dead at the outset goes as follows:

Customer 'what do you charge for a bunch of flowers?'

Salesperson 'we start at £X'

Customer 'I'll have one.'

Easy, isn't it? No argument, no fuss, no persuasion, no doubts (at that moment), no effort. But if you could somehow project yourself into that customer's mind subsequent to this sale he will possibly be thinking along these lines:

'Well that was a quick sale and no mistake, but I would have liked a chance to explain what these flowers are for. Wonder why he (or she) didn't offer me anything else; why didn't he suggest I had a look around, take a bit of interest in me – after all, I'm the one who is paying and I didn't really mind what it cost, within reason of course, so long as I got something nice. At least he could have said hello and goodbye or thankyou, but he just stood there. It wasn't as if he was deeply involved in doing anything else; come to think of it, there was no one else in the shop and I don't wonder either.'

There was once a popular song called 'Accentuate the positive' and although the words and music were probably not to everyone's taste, the sentiment behind it was obvious.

How much more satisfactory if the scenario had begun with 'good morning, how are you today?' Or something similar, for this immediately opens the door to dialogue, giving the potential customer the opportunity to reply in either a major or minor key. He may actually be feeling very down, cross or otherwise rather anti-social, and might welcome the chance to complain to someone. And even if he has an open mind, is neutral, so to speak, being neither very down nor particularly exhilarated, a smiling welcome costs nothing.

The opening gambit is all-important for it opens the door to negotiation. Whether or not a long discussion ensues is up to the customer. If he is a person of few words, your 'sales antennae' should quickly register the fact; if discussion seems to be going on too long, it is up to you to guide it towards decision-making. Decision, that is as to 'what'. The 'how much' still should come later. For it is during discussion that you will get small clues as to the cost-level of the transaction. And remember, once a price is quoted and agreed, you cannot deviate from it unless the customer definitely changes his mind, asks for more flowers, or more expensive ones, or maybe a bigger arrangement.

That is the deadly pitfall, the sale-stopper, of the words 'we start at £X'. You have pinpointed a price and, human nature being what it is, everyone hopes to get more for the money and pay less for it! Therefore if you are asked the direct question 'what do you charge?' there really is no way of avoiding a direct answer, yet it can be done in such a way as still to leave open the possibility of price-negotiation. So your reply can be something on the lines of 'we can make a bunch of flowers for almost any price; do you have any special flowers in mind?'

Sales persuasion

This must not be confused with high-pressure selling. You are not trying to persuade the customer that he needs flowers, for by coming into your shop, he has already established that fact. Your role as the firm's representative on the sales floor, is to make sure the customer gets, as near as humanly possible, what he has in mind. For he may be expecting too much for his money. Unfortunately not everyone buys flowers regularly and so they remain blissfully unaware that this commodity is just as affected by rising costs in every sector – raw materials, production, transport, distribution – as any other consumer goods.

If his spending power is firmly fixed, take time to explain what he can have for that amount of cash. Be sympathetic, clarify just what is available in his particular price bracket. After all, he is bound to appreciate that costs vary for the commodity, for surely no one would expect to get a colour televison for the same price as a transistor radio.

But never, never appear to be snobbish over the cash level of the sale. For very likely the customer who buys small today and emerges from your shop feeling satisfied with all aspects of the deal, will surely return later to become one of your most regular clients. Which would you prefer? A client who, regularly, once each week, buys one red rose, or the person who appears once each year for 10 of the same roses? The economics are obvious.

The other side of the coin It is a real challenge when the client says 'I want something extra special; never mind what it costs'. This, too, has its pitfalls. For most people do, in fact, care about cost at whatever level, so this particular situation can be yet another trap for the unwary. Dialogue is of the utmost importance here, for it will be the means of helping to shed light on the nub of the order; for example, the occasion and possibly, also, one or two of the many reasons why, so far as cost is concerned, the sky's the limit.

It may well be that any design you make at whatever cost will be agreeable, but in most instances, there is, in fact, a limit, even though it could actually be in the client's subconscious. So, before allowing your artistic and business impulses to race ahead, it is just as well to seek some clarification. Try to steer the customer towards giving you a figure – not the other way round. For it might – just might – be less than he had in mind. Alternatively, propose a flexible price bracket to within an agreed sum which is high enough for you to do the order justice yet which gives you space to manoeuvre should it be necessary.

Both salesperson and client are then moving towards the perfect balance of customer satisfaction and a logical transaction.

Special occasion selling
Sympathy flowers These can range from an informal modestly-priced funeral spray to all the tributes for a big funeral. People's attitudes vary tremendously when placing this kind of order. Some are very business-like, having previously held a family conference. Everything is listed; the type of tributes wanted,

possibly even the cost and the message for each card.

Others are understandably confused and disorientated. It may be tactful to make a few notes, show them pictures of a selection of designs and suggest that they make their decision at home and either call back or telephone the order. It is also tactful, when the card messages have not been written, to give the customer some blanks, so that they can be written in privacy.

But however distressed the client may seem at this moment it does not follow that they are unaware of your tact and sales ability. Most likely they will be the first to register appreciation after the event, either in a note of thanks or by coming to thank you in person. This really is a rewarding situation, for then you know that not only have the tributes brought solace at a time of sadness, but also that in yet another sphere, you achieved that delicate balance of sales satisfaction between client and shop.

The wedding order Probably the most challenging and exciting of all types of order, yet even so, one that can contain many pitfalls for the unwary or incompetent salesperson. However, initially the most important thing is to smile, to listen and to look interested. Your prospective client, and very likely her mother as well, will understandably be enthusiastic, so let that enthusiasm brush off on you.

Naturally there are a number of details that must be noted, date and time of ceremony being the most important, but do not, at this early stage just reach for the order book, pencil poised. Some brides already know exactly what they want, for their own bouquet and also for the bridesmaids; others have no fixed ideas. You will show some examples, in pictures as well as actual designs in fabric flowers, invite her to hold them, thus forming an idea of relative size, colour and shape.

Meanwhile, information will emerge in conversation, without direct questions as to the number of bridesmaids, the style of the dresses, where the reception will be held and the general picture takes shape. If dress patterns are produced, be sure to admire them saying it will definitely be the prettiest wedding of the year.

At this stage it is a good idea to produce the wedding order form, for certainly the date and time, number of bridesmaids are details that can quickly be noted. Take the order in duplicate, so that one copy is filed in your special wedding order book and the second copy can be handed to the bride so that she is in no doubt as to what she has ordered, what has been paid for and how much of the cost is outstanding.

At the same time, never appear to be rushing a decision. If you sense uncertainty in getting down to specifics so far as designs are concerned, make a few suggestions so that the bride can, perhaps, have time at home to formulate her ideas. A give-away design brochure is most useful in this respect and frequently saves a lot of time in the shop.

So far the discussions usually encompass the actual wedding designs, head-dresses, corsages and buttonholes. Church arrangements and reception designs will possibly involve a visit so that an estimate can be prepared. Try to arrange that this is done as promptly as possible.

On the subject of salesmanship in general, it is admittedly all very well to read about it in theory, but quite another matter to carry those theories into practice. For no one can visualise every possible situation, nor make allowances for every kind of eventuality. So at best, theories are but generalisations, guidelines that can be adopted; not rules to be slavishly followed, regardless of human reaction.

There are some who are natural salespersons; others do not have this gift, yet no one knows till they try. Some people literally shrink from contact with the general public, yet they are brilliant on the telephone. Others are far more use to the firm doing routine work in the background, for it certainly does not follow that every good florist is a good salesperson – or the reverse.

Therefore it is absolutely vital that the administration is able to evaluate a person's strong or weak areas, instead of blindly pushing them into positions for which they are unsuited; square pegs in round holes, so to speak. For not only will the staff as a whole enjoy greater job satisfaction, but the general efficiency of the whole organisation will eventually be on a far higher plane.

19 Peak trading days

Christmas time	– world wide	
New Year's Day	– world wide	
St Valentine's Day	– world wide – 14 February	
Easter	– world wide	
Mothers' Day (Mothering Sunday)		
	Britain	– third Sunday before Easter
	USA	– 8 May
	France	– 29 May
	Germany	– 8 May
	Spain	– first Sunday in May
	Italy	– second Sunday in May
	Denmark	– second Sunday in May
	Finland	– second Sunday in May
	Holland	– second Sunday in May
	Norway	– second Sunday in February
	Sweden	– 29 May
	Belgium	– second Sunday in May
Father's Day	– third Sunday in June	

France	Lily-of-the-Valley Day	1 May
Germany	All-Saints	– 1 November
Spain	All-Saints	– 1 November
Italy	Woman's Day	– 8 March
	Fathers' Day	– 19 March
Denmark	Fathers' Day	– 5 June
Finland	Fathers' Day	– second Sunday in November
Holland	Fathers' Day	– third Sunday in June
Norway	Fathers' Day	– second Sunday in November
	National Day	– 17 May
	Memorial Day	– first Sunday in November
Sweden	Fathers' Day	– 13 November
Belgium	Lily-of-the-Valley Day	– 1 May
	Memorial Day	– 30 May
	Fathers' Day	– second Sunday in June
	Day of the Sick	– 18 July
Israel	*Purim	– February/March
	*Passover Eve	– March/April

Israel		
continued	Mothers' Day	– 13 February
	Memorial Day	– 10 April
	*Rosh Hashanah Eve	– 7 September
	*Chanukah	– December
USA	St Patrick's Day	– 17 March
	Passover	– 29 March
	Secretaries' Day	– 27 April
	Memorial Day	– 28 May
	Fathers' Day	– 19 June
	Independence Day	– 4 July
	Grandparents' Day	– 11 September
	Labour Day	– 3 September
	Rosh Hashanah	– 8 September
	Yom Kippur	– 17 September
	Sweetest Day	– 15 October
	Mother-in-laws' Day	– 23 October
	Thanksgiving Day	– 22 November

Some dates are religious, some traditional and others are special national holidays. There is no occasion that is not enhanced with flowers. Since international communications are forever increasing, it is useful for the florist to know some dates, or the approximate time of year when peak trading times occur in other countries.

*Dates may vary depending on the lunar calendar.

20 Questions and answers

Q How can I train to be a florist?

A By taking formal courses, either long-term residential or an intensive short course: by training with a qualified florist: by working with a qualified florist and going to day-release classes.

Q What does 'qualified' mean?

A It means that the florist has attained a specific standard of efficiency as established by the national examinations of the particular country.

Q Do standards vary in other countries?

A Examination requirements are different because design styles vary from one country to another. This is one reason why florists should try to widen their experience by working overseas.

Q Is there any organisation in Great Britain that can give me information on the flower industry?

A Yes, the Society of Floristry and the British Retail Florists' Association, also the National Examinations Board (with the City and Guilds of London Institute).

Q Are there any trade papers available?

A The Florist: the Retail Flower Trades Journal, The Complete Florist.

Q As a student, how much can I expect to earn?

A It depends on your previous experience; on how much (if any) pre-training you have had; on your school-leaving examination passes; also on the area in which you work. Most employers pay on the basis of ability and merit, not on age.

Q How can I learn salesmanship if I have never worked in a shop?

A   First by learning as much as possible about what you are selling; by knowing current prices; by watching and listening to senior sales staff; by evaluating how you are treated in other shops; if you were happy with this treatment and if not, why not? Salesmanship, incidentally, includes your telephone personality.

Q   Is it better to aim at having my own shop rather than working as a hired hand?

A   This depends on the individual. Some people thrive on the challenge of responsibility; others are at their best working under direction. Before opening a shop, you should gain as much experience as possible in different types of shops; city shop, country town shop, garden centre, as well as overseas. You will probably also need some business training.

Q   On leaving school, is it better to go straight into a workroom or first attend formal courses?

A   This depends on a number of factors. The ideal situation is first to go to formal classes, then into a workroom and then to advanced formal classes for further training.

Q   Which subjects will help towards a successful career in floristry?

A   English; biology; mathematics; at least one foreign language; geography; art or handicraft will all come in useful. Broadly speaking, no school subject is irrelevant to the flower industry and any, or all of them, eventually contribute towards a mature and balanced personality.

Q   What are the basic qualifications necessary for me to be accepted as a trainee florist?

A   Prospective employers usually rate personality above academic qualifications: thus, you should speak well: dress neatly: walk and move well: have legible neat handwriting; be willing to work hard and be cheerful. Also some examination passes (those coveted 'pieces of paper') will obviously be an added plus in your favour.

Q   What prospects are there for men in retail floristry?

A   The prospects are good. It is far more demanding than many other careers. One needs considerable strength and good health to be a florist, as well as good co-ordination, patience of a particular brand, tenacity, flexibility of outlook and a good sense of business. Being a retail florist is as interesting and challenging for a man as for a woman.

Q Will life in a retail shop seem unduly restrictive?

A Not at all. You will have continual contact with people from every walk of life. Also by developing an interest in the industry as a whole there will be ample opportunity for contacts outside the shop.

Q What is the point of taking examinations in commercial floristry and horticulture?

A The standards are recognised both nationally and internationally. The certificates indicate that you have measured up to these standards, not only in quality of work but also from the time factor angle.

Some horticultural knowledge is of great value to the florist, giving a deeper understanding of flowers and increased sensitivity to their qualities and needs.

Index

Address labels 134
Advance orders 167
All-round design 45
Analogous harmony 22, 25
Anemones 74
Anniversaries 51
Arrangements 40, 83
Asters 74
Asymmetrical design 46, 47
Axis 19

Backing 46
Balance 14, 20, 41
Ball point pen 6
Bascade/baskette 94, 134
Bases 54
Bouquet bases 85
    bridal 87
    classic or shower 89
    handles 85
Box pleating 63
Bulb flowers 117
Butterfly bow 128, 129

Cake top 87, 98
Camellia 61
Calyx 34
Candle cup 12, 50
Candles 12, 50
Cards, greeting 12, 58
    flower care 13
Care of stock 114–120
Carmen rose 97
Cash point 167

Cellophane presentation 126,
    129
Circlet head-dresses 82
Chaplet 76
Chlorophytum 30
Chrysanthemum 57, 115
Church arrangements 101
Cleaning, routine 144
Coffee 13
Colonial posy 98
Colour symbolism 23
    wheel 19, 20, 23
Complaints, dealing with 154
Complementary harmony 22, 24
Conditioning flowers 142
Cones (tubes) 50
Containers 41, 144
Cool storage 120
Corsage boxes 12
Corsages 78, 80
Cross, open 68
Cushion 71
Customer relations 152

Daffodil 49, 74
Dahlia 74, 117
Damage 149
Decorative form 49
Delivery lists 139
Deliveries 126, 147
    organising 146–57
Delphinium 20
Design, technical 16
    visual 16

Display 107, 110
  shop 143
Distinction 41
Double-ended spray 59
Double internal wiring 32
Double leg mount 34, 68
Dry pack 120
Duchesse rose 97
Duster 6

Easter 12, 43, 110
Economy 43
Envelopes 12
Equilateral triangle 18
Everlastings 83
Extra help 166, 168

Fidelity 160
Fixing tape 41
Flower ball 96
  food 11
  spheres 104
  trees 104
  form groups 28
Foam, floral 11, 42, 65
  dry 11
Formal designs 61
Freesia 36
Funeral tributes 54–75
  spray 56

Gates of Heaven 71
Gerbera 42, 115
German pins 63
Gift wrap 50
Gladioli 42, 57
Glue gum 51
Grouping 40

Heart, foam-based 73
  moss-based 73
Holidays 159
Hook method 31, 36
Hyacinth 74, 96
Hydrangea 74

Head-dresses 78, 87
Holly 77
Hospital arrangements 48

Impact 40
Informal tribute 55
Internal wiring 31
Iris 49
Isosceles triangle 18

Kleenex 41, 42
Knife 6, 115

Laurel 61, 77
  pinning 75
Leafshine 76
Lighting 111
Lily-of-the-valley 35, 115
Loop method 61
Logo 7
Lunch breaks 144, 145

Masking 42, 48
Monochromatic harmony 22, 24
Moss 10
Mossed bases 65, 66
Mossing 55
Moss, Icelandic or reindeer 84
Mothers' Day 12, 110, 165, 169
Mount wire 28
Multi-loop bow 127, 128

Narcissi 74
Natural bunch 52
Non-delivery, 148
Notebook 6

Oasis-fix 11, 12, 41, 42, 51, 103
Oasis-tape 16
Open Book 74
Open posy 96
Orchids 37, 80, 119
Order pads 13
Order checking 140
Outline 19, 20

Outside decorations 101
Overalls 7

Packing, cut flowers 126
  container designs 130
Parallel form 48
Paper clips 13
Peak trading days 117
Pens 13
Pew sprays 192
Philodendron 30
Pins 12, 13, 65
Pillow 71
Poinsettia 115
Point of origin 18
Pomander 100, 135
Posy, bridal 31, 85
  colonial 98
  open 96
  pad 60
  Victorian 45, 99
  wreath 60
Prayer Book spray 81
Presentation 125–30
Price tickets 109
Profile 20
Prongs 11, 41, 59
Proportion 44
Publicity 164

Raffia 53
Ranunculus 74
Recession 40
Records 163
Refreshments 7
Repetition 40
Requisition list 13
Ribbon bow 58, 94
  edging 62
Ribbons 12
Roses 37, 49, 117
Rose leaves 30
  pinning 34
Routine cleaning of shop 144

Salesmanship 171–74
Saturday Special 46
Scabious 74
Scindapsus 30
Scissors 6, 115
Selling, special occasion 174
Sellotape 16, 85
Semi-crescent design 90
Sheaves 60
Shoes 7
Silver reel wire 35, 36, 94, 95, 96
Split complementary harmony
  25
Sprayer 41
Spray chrysanthemum 31, 74
Stability 16
Staff relations 157–58
Stem texture groups 28
Stephanotis 30, 35, 36, 117
Stitch method 29
Stock 74
Storage, cool 120
String 10
Sugar 13
Symmetry 46
Sympathy basket 56, 58
  work method 58
Sympathy designs 54

Taping 28
Tape-splitting 28
Tape, florists 10
Telephone 142, 166
Texture 19, 23
Tradescantia 30
Triadic harmony 22, 26
Top spray 68
Tubes (cones) 50

Unit assembly 38, 82

Vacant chair 55, 71
Vacations 159
Vehicle responsibility 149

Vegetative form 49
Vending machines 159
Victorian posy 45, 99
Violets 74

Weddings 85
Window dressing 107
Wire 6, 9, 10
Wire frames 10

Wires, green 37
Wiring methods 27–38
Work routine 137–44
Working clothes 7
Wrapping paper 12
Wreath 70

Zebrina 30

Other relevant titles

The Successful Florist
Stanley Coleman

Grateful thanks must be given to Mr Coleman for the timely arrival of this textbook when our industry is once again going through a period of great change and with a knowledge based on the book and commonsense and experience, will set the reader up to cope with the future.
British Retail Florists' Association House Magazine

Dictionary of Floristry and Flower Arranging
Anthony Gatrell

Here at last is a reference book bulging with clear and concise information on Flower Arranging. Floristry, Botany and Horticulture terms. This compact, hard-backed dictionary fills a much needed gap in the flower arranger's library . . . In alphabetical order and with 350 splendid line drawings specially prepared by the author, this book will become indispensable for any serious flower arranger. It will be particularly valuable to City and Guilds Flower Arranging/Floristry students as well as teachers and judges of the subject.
    It is rare to find a book of this type written solely for the Flower Arranger/Florist. Buy it. *Insight*

Flower Arranger's Garden
Griselda Maurice

Flower Arranger's Guide to Showing
Howard Franklin

Flower Arranger's A–Z
Daphne Vagg

Flower Arrangements: Month by Month
Julia Clements

Details of these titles and other books on flower arranging and horticulture are available on request from
B T Batsford Limited
4 Fitzhardinge Street
London W1H 0AH